SOME MISTAKES OF MOSES

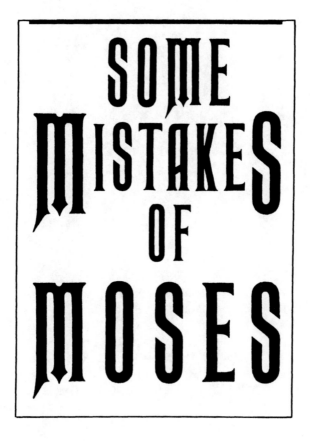

SOME MISTAKES OF MOSES

ROBERT INGERSOLL

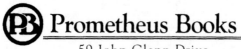 Prometheus Books

59 John Glenn Drive
Amherst, New York 14228-2197

Published 1986 by
Prometheus Books
59 John Glenn Drive
Amherst, New York 14228–2197
VOICE: 716–691–0133, ext. 207
FAX: 716–691–0137
WWW.PROMETHEUSBOOKS.COM

ISBN 0–87975–361–7

Printed in the United States of America on acid-free paper.

TO

MRS. SUE. M. FARRELL,

IN LAW MY SISTER,

AND IN FACT MY FRIEND,

THIS VOLUME,

AS A TOKEN OF RESPECT AND LOVE

IS DEDICATED.

PREFACE.

—

For many years I have regarded the Pentateuch simply as a record of a barbarous people, in which are found a great number of the ceremonies of savagery, many absurd and unjust laws, and thousands of ideas inconsistent with known and demonstrated facts. To me it seemed almost a crime to teach that this record was written by inspired men; that slavery, polygamy, wars of conquest and extermination were right, and that there was a time when men could win the approbation of infinite Intelligence, Justice, and Mercy, by violating maidens and by butchering babes. To me it seemed more reasonable that savage men had made these laws; and I endeavored in a lecture, entitled " Some Mistakes of Moses," to point out some of the errors, contradictions, and impossibilities contained in the Pentateuch. The lecture was never written and consequently never delivered twice the same. On several occasions it was reported and published without consent, and without revision. All these publications were grossly and glaringly incorrect. As published, they have been answered several hundred times, and many of the clergy are still engaged in the great work. To keep these reverend gentlemen from wasting their talents on the mistakes of reporters and printers, I concluded to publish the principal points in all my lectures on this subject. And here, it may be proper for me to say, that arguments cannot be answered by personal abuse ; that there is no logic in slander, and that falsehood, in the long run, defeats itself. People who love their enemies should, at least, tell the truth about their friends. Should it turn out that I am the worst man in the whole world, the story of the flood will remain just as improbable as before, and the contradictions of the Pentateuch will still demand an explanation.

There was a time when a falsehood, fulminated from the pulpit, smote like a sword ; but, the supply having greatly exceeded the demand, clerical misrepresentation has at last become almost an innocent amusement. Remembering that only a few years ago men, women, and even children, were imprisoned, tortured and burned, for having expressed in an exceedingly mild and gentle way, the ideas entertained by me, I congratulate myself that calumny is now the pulpit's last resort. The old instruments of torture are kept only to gratify curiosity ; the chains are rusting away, and the demolition of time has allowed even the dungeons of the Inquisition to be visited by light. The church, impotent and malicious, regrets, not the abuse, but the loss of her power, and seeks to hold by falsehood what she gained by cruelty and force, by fire and fear. Christianity cannot live in peace with any other form of faith. If that religion be true, there is but one savior, one inspired book, and but one little narrow grass-grown path that leads to heaven. Such a religion is necessarily uncompromising,

unreasoning, aggressive and insolent. Christianity
has held all other creeds and forms in infinite contempt, divided the world into enemies and friends,
and verified the awful declaration of its founder—a
declaration that wet with blood the sword he came to
bring, and made the horizon of a thousand years
lurid with the fagots' flames.

Too great praise challenges attention, and often
brings to light a thousand faults that otherwise the
general eye would never see. Were we allowed to
read the Bible as we do all other books, we would
admire its beauties, treasure its worthy thoughts,
and account for all its absurd, grotesque and cruel
things, by saying that its authors lived in rude,
barbaric times. But we are told that it was written
by inspired men ; that it contains the will of God ;
that it is perfect, pure, and true in all its parts ; the
source and standard of all moral and religious truth ;
that it is the star and anchor of all human hope ; the
only guide for man, the only torch in Nature's night.
These claims are so at variance with every known
recorded fact, so palpably absurd, that every free,

unbiased soul is forced to raise the standard of revolt.

We read the pagan sacred books with profit and delight. With myth and fable we are ever charmed, and find a pleasure in the endless repetition of the beautiful, poetic, and absurd. We find, in all these records of the past, philosophies and dreams, and efforts stained with tears, of great and tender souls who tried to pierce the mystery of life and death, to answer the eternal questions of the Whence and Whither, and vainly sought to make, with bits of shattered glass, a mirror that would, in very truth, reflect the face and form of Nature's perfect self.

These myths were born of hopes, and fears, and tears, and smiles, and they were touched and colored by all there is of joy and grief between the rosy dawn of birth, and death's sad night. They clothed even the stars with passion, and gave to gods the faults and frailties of the sons of men. In them, the winds and waves were music, and all the lakes, and streams, and springs,—the mountains, woods and perfumed dells were haunted by a thousand fairy

forms.   They thrilled the veins of Spring with trem-
ulous desire ; made tawny Summer's billowed breast
the throne and home of love; filled Autumn's arms
with sun-kissed grapes, and gathered sheaves ; and
pictured Winter as a weak old king who felt, like
Lear upon his withered face, Cordelia's tears.
These myths, though false, are beautiful, and have
for many ages and in countless ways, enriched the
heart and kindled thought.   But if the world were
taught that all these things are true and all inspired
of God, and that eternal punishment will be the lot
of him who dares deny or doubt, the sweetest myth
of all the Fable World would lose its beauty, and
become a scorned and hateful thing to every brave
and thoughtful man.

Robert G. Ingersoll.

Washington, D. C., *Oct. 7th, 1879.*

CONTENTS.

SOME MISTAKES OF MOSES.

———

HE WHO ENDEAVORS TO CONTROL THE MIND BY FORCE
IS A TYRANT, AND HE WHO SUBMITS IS A SLAVE.

I.

I WANT to do what little I can to make my country truly free, to broaden the intellectual horizon of our people, to destroy the prejudices born of ignorance and fear, to do away with the blind worship of the ignoble past, with the idea that all the great and good are dead, that the living are totally depraved, that all pleasures are sins, that sighs and groans are alone pleasing to God, that thought is dangerous, that intellectual courage is a crime, that cowardice is a virtue, that a certain belief is necessary to secure salvation, that to carry a cross in this world will give us a palm in the next, and that we must allow some priest to be the pilot of our souls.

Until every soul is freely permitted to investigate every book, and creed, and dogma for itself, the world cannot be free. Mankind will be enslaved until there is mental grandeur enough to allow each man to have his thought and say. This earth will be a paradise when men can, upon all these questions differ, and yet grasp each other's hands as friends. It is amazing to me that a difference of opinion upon subjects that we know nothing with certainty about, should make us hate, persecute, and despise each other. Why a difference of opinion upon predestination, or the Trinity, should make people imprison and burn each other seems beyond the comprehension of man ; and yet in all countries where Christians have existed, they have destroyed each other to the exact extent of their power. Why should a believer in God hate an atheist? Surely the atheist has not injured God, and surely he is human, capable of joy and pain, and entitled to all the rights of man. Would it not be far better to treat this atheist, at least, as well as he treats us?

Christians tell me that they love their enemies, and yet all I ask is—not that they love their enemies, not that they love their friends even, but that they treat those who differ from them, with simple fairness.

We do not wish to be forgiven, but we wish Christians to so act that we will not have to forgive them.

If all will admit that all have an equal right to
think, then the question is forever solved; but as
long as organized and powerful churches, pretending
to hold the keys of heaven and hell, denounce every
person as an outcast and criminal who thinks for
himself and denies their authority, the world will
be filled with hatred and suffering. To hate man
and worship God seems to be the sum of all the
creeds.

That which has happened in most countries has
happened in ours. When a religion is founded, the
educated, the powerful—that is to say, the priests
and nobles, tell the ignorant and superstitious—that
is to say, the people, that the religion of their country
was given to their fathers by God himself; that it is
the only true religion; that all others were conceived
in falsehood and brought forth in fraud, and that all
who believe in the true religion will be happy forever, while all others will burn in hell. For the
purpose of governing the people, that is to say, for
the purpose of being supported by the people, the
priests and nobles declare this religion to be sacred,
and that whoever adds to, or takes from it, will be

burned here by man, and hereafter by God. The
result of this is, that the priests and nobles will not
allow the people to change ; and when, after a time,
the priests, having intellectually advanced, wish to
take a step in the direction of progress, the people
will not allow them to change. At first, the rabble
are enslaved by the priests, and afterwards the rabble
become the masters.

One of the first things I wish to do, is to free the
orthodox clergy. I am a great friend of theirs, and
in spite of all they may say against me, I am going
to do them a great and lasting service. Upon their
necks are visible the marks of the collar, and upon
their backs those of the lash. They are not allowed
to read and think for themselves. They are taught
like parrots, and the best are those who repeat, with
the fewest mistakes, the sentences they have been
taught. They sit like owls upon some dead limb of
the tree of knowledge, and hoot the same old hoots
that have been hooted for eighteen hundred years.
Their congregations are not grand enough, nor
sufficiently civilized, to be willing that the poor
preachers shall think for themselves. They are not
employed for that purpose. Investigation is regarded
as a dangerous experiment, and the ministers are

warned that none of that kind of work will be tolerated. They are notified to stand by the old creed, and to avoid all original thought, as a mortal pestilence. Every minister is employed like an attorney—either for plaintiff or defendant,—and he is expected to be true to his client. If he changes his mind, he is regarded as a deserter, and denounced, hated, and slandered accordingly. Every orthodox clergyman agrees not to change. He contracts not to find new facts, and makes a bargain that he will deny them if he does. Such is the position of a Protestant minister in this nineteenth century. His condition excites my pity; and to better it, I am going to do what little I can.

Some of the clergy have the independence to break away, and the intellect to maintain themselves as free men, but the most are compelled to submit to the dictation of the orthodox, and the dead. They are not employed to give their thoughts, but simply to repeat the ideas of others. They are not expected to give even the doubts that may suggest themselves, but are required to walk in the narrow, verdureless path trodden by the ignorance of the past. The forests and fields on either side are nothing to them. They must not even look at the purple hills, t.or pause to hear the babble of the brooks. They must remain in the dusty road where the guide-boards are. They must confine themselves to the "fall of man," the expulsion from the garden, the "scheme of salvation," the "second birth," the atonement, the happiness of the redeemed, and the misery of the lost. They must be careful not to express any new ideas upon these great questions. It is much safer for them to quote from the works of the dead. The more vividly they describe the sufferings of the unregenerate, of those who attended theatres and balls, and drank wine in summer gardens on the Sabbath-day, and laughed at priests, the better ministers they are supposed to be. They must show that misery fits the good for heaven, while happiness prepares the bad for hell; that the wicked get all their good things in this life, and the good all their evil; that in this world God punishes the people he loves, and in the next, the ones he hates; that happiness makes us bad here, but not in heaven; that pain makes us good here, but not in hell. No matter how absurd these things may appear to the carnal mind, they must be preached and they must be believed. If they were reasonable, there would be no virtue in believing. Even the publicans and sinners believe reasonable things. To believe without evidence, or in spite of it, is accounted as righteousness to the sincere and humble Christian.

The ministers are in duty bound to denounce all intellectual pride, and show that we are never quite so dear to God as when we admit that we are poor, corrupt and idiotic worms ; that we never should have been born ; that we ought to be damned without the least delay ; that we are so infamous that we like to enjoy ourselves ; that we love our wives and children better than our God ; that we are generous only because we are vile ; that we are honest from the meanest motives, and that sometimes we have fallen so low that we have had doubts about the inspiration of the Jewish Scriptures. In short, they are expected to denounce all pleasant paths and rustling trees, to curse the grass and flowers, and glorify the dust and weeds. They are expected to malign the wicked people in the green and happy fields, who sit and laugh beside the gurgling springs or climb the hills and wander as they will. They are expected to point out the dangers of freedom, the safety of implicit obedience, and to show the wickedness of philosophy, the goodness of faith, the immorality of science and the purity of ignorance.

Now and then a few pious people discover some young man of a religious turn of mind and a consumptive habit of body, not quite sickly enough to die, nor healthy enough to be wicked. The idea occurs to them that he would make a good orthodox minister. They take up a contribution, and send the young man to some theological school where he can be taught to repeat a creed and despise reason. Should it turn out that the young man had some mind of his own, and, after graduating, should change his opinions and preach a different doctrine from that taught in the school, every man who contributed a dollar towards his education would feel that he had been robbed, and would denounce him as a dishonest and ungrateful wretch.

The pulpit should not be a pillory. Congregations should allow the minister a little liberty. They should, at least, permit him to tell the truth.

They have, in Massachusetts, at a place called Andover, a kind of minister factory, where each professor takes an oath once in five years—that time being considered the life of an oath—that he has not, during the last five years, and will not, during the next five years, intellectually advance. There is probably no oath that they could easier keep. Prob-

ably, since the foundation stone of that institution
was laid there has not been a single case of perjury.
The old creed is still taught.   They still insist that
God is infinitely wise, powerful and good, and that
all men are totally depraved.   They insist that the
best man God ever made, deserved to be damned
the moment he was finished.   Andover ʼputs its brand
upon every minister it turns out, the same as Shef-
field and Birmingham brand their wares, and all who
see the brand know exactly what the minister believes, the books he has read, the arguments he
relies on, and just what he intellectually is.   They
know just what he can be depended on to preach,
and that he will continue to shrink and shrivel, and
grow solemnly stupid day by day until he reaches
the Andover of the grave and becomes truly orthodox forever.

I have not singled out the Andover factory
because it is worse than the others.   They are all
about the same.   The professors, for the most part,
are ministers who failed in the pulpit and were retired
to the seminary on account of their deficiency in
reason and their excess of faith.   As a rule, they
know nothing of this world, and far less of the next ;
but they have the power of stating the most absurd

propositions with faces solemn as stupidity touched
by fear.

Something should be done for the liberation of
these men. They should be allowed to grow—to
have sunlight and air. They should no longer be
chained and tied to confessions of faith, to mouldy
books and musty creeds. Thousands of ministers
are anxious to give their honest thoughts. The
hands of wives and babes now stop their mouths.
They must have bread, and so the husbands and
fathers are forced to preach a doctrine that they hold
in scorn. For the sake of shelter, food and clothes,
they are obliged to defend the childish miracles of the
past, and denounce the sublime discoveries of to-day.
They are compelled to attack all modern thought, to
point out the dangers of science, the wickedness of
investigation and the corrupting influence of logic.
It is for them to show that virtue rests upon
ignorance and faith, while vice impudently feeds and
fattens upon fact and demonstration. It is a part of
their business to malign and vilify the Voltaires,
Humes, Paines, Humboldts, Tyndalls, Haeckels,
Darwins, Spencers, and Drapers, and to bow with
uncovered heads before the murderers, adulterers,
and persecutors of the world. They are, for the

most part, engaged in poisoning the minds of the young, prejudicing children against science, teaching the astronomy and geology of the Bible, and inducing all to desert the sublime standard of reason.

These orthodox ministers do not add to the sum of knowledge. They produce nothing. They live upon alms. They hate laughter and joy. They officiate at weddings, sprinkle water upon babes, and utter meaningless words and barren promises above the dead. They laugh at the agony of unbelievers, mock at their tears, and of their sorrows make a jest. There are some noble exceptions. Now and then a pulpit holds a brave and honest man. Their congregations are willing that they should think—willing that their ministers should have a little freedom.

As we become civilized, more and more liberty will be accorded to these men, until finally ministers will give their best and highest thoughts. The congregations will finally get tired of hearing about the patriarchs and saints, the miracles and wonders, and will insist upon knowing something about the men and women of our day, and the accomplishments and discoveries of our time. They will finally insist upon knowing how to escape the evils of this world instead of the next. They will ask light upon the

enigmas of this life. They will wish to know what
we shall do with our criminals instead of what God
will do with his—how we shall do away with beggary
and want—with crime and misery—with prostitution,
disease and famine,—with tyranny in all its cruel
forms—with prisons and scaffolds, and how we shall
reward the honest workers, and fill the world with
happy homes! These are the problems for the
pulpits and congregations of an enlightened future.
If Science cannot finally answer these questions, it is
a vain and worthless thing.

The clergy, however, will continue to answer
them in the old way, until their congregations are
good enough to set them free. They will still talk
about believing in the Lord Jesus Christ, as though
that were the only remedy for all human ills. They
will still teach that retrogression is the only path
that leads to light; that we must go back, that faith
is the only sure guide, and that reason is a delusive
glare, lighting only the road to eternal pain.

Until the clergy are free they cannot be intellectually honest. We can never tell what they really
believe until they know that they can safely speak.
They console themselves now by a secret resolution
to be as liberal as they dare, with the hope that they

can finally educate their congregations to the point of allowing them to think a little for themselves. They hardly know what they ought to do. The best part of their lives has been wasted in studying subjects of no possible value. Most of them are married, have families, and know but one way of making their living. Some of them say that if they do not preach these foolish dogmas, others will, and that they may through fear, after all, restrain mankind. Besides, they hate publicly to admit that they are mistaken, that the whole thing is a delusion, that the "scheme of salvation" is absurd, and that the Bible is no better than some other books, and worse than most.

You can hardly expect a bishop to leave his palace, or the pope to vacate the Vatican. As long as people want popes, plenty of hypocrites will be found to take the place. And as long as labor fatigues, there will be found a good many men willing to preach once a week, if other folks will work and give them bread. In other words, while the demand lasts, the supply will never fail.

If the people were a little more ignorant, astrology would flourish—if a little more enlightened, religion would perish!

II.

FREE SCHOOLS.

IT is also my desire to free the schools. When a
professor in a college finds a fact, he should make
it known, even if it is inconsistent with something
Moses said. Public opinion must not compel the
professor to hide a fact, and, "like the base Indian,
throw the pearl away." With the single exception
of Cornell, there is not a college in the United States
where truth has ever been a welcome guest. The
moment one of the teachers denies the inspiration of
the Bible, he is discharged. If he discovers a fact
inconsistent with that book, so much the worse for
the fact, and especially for the discoverer of the fact.
He must not corrupt the minds of his pupils with
demonstrations. He must beware of every truth
that cannot, in some way be made to harmonize with
the superstitions of the Jews. Science has nothing
in common with religion. Facts and miracles nevei

did, and never will agree. They are not in the least related. They are deadly foes. What has religion to do with facts? Nothing. Can there be Methodist mathematics, Catholic astronomy, Presbyterian geology, Baptist biology, or Episcopal botany? Why, then, should a sectarian college exist? Only that which somebody knows should be taught in our schools. We should not collect taxes to pay people for guessing. The common school is the bread of life for the people, and it should not be touched by the withering hand of superstition.

Our country will never be filled with great institutions of learning until there is an absolute divorce between Church and School. As long as the mutilated records of a barbarous people are placed by priest and professor above the reason of mankind, we shall reap but little benefit from church or school.

Instead of dismissing professors for finding something out, let us rather discharge those who do not. Let each teacher understand that investigation is not dangerous for him; that his bread is safe, no matter how much truth he may discover, and that his salary will not be reduced, simply because he finds that the ancient Jews did not know the entire history of the world.

Besides, it is not fair to make the Catholic support a Protestant school, nor is it just to collect taxes
from infidels and atheists to support schools in which
any system of religion is taught.

The sciences are not sectarian. People do not
persecute each other on account of disagreements in
mathematics. Families are not divided about botany,
and astronomy does not even tend to make a man
hate his father and mother. It is what people do not
know, that they persecute each other about. Science
will bring, not a sword, but peace.

Just as long as religion has control of the schools,
science will be an outcast. Let us free our institutions of learning. Let us dedicate them to the
science of eternal truth. Let us tell every teacher
to ascertain all the facts he can—to give us light, to
follow Nature, no matter where she leads; to be
infinitely true to himself and us; to feel that he is
without a chain, except the obligation to be honest;
that he is bound by no books, by no creed, neither
by the sayings of the dead nor of the living; that
that he is asked to look with his own eyes, to
reason for himself without fear, to investigate in
every possible direction, and to bring us the fruit of
all his work.

At present, a good many men engaged in scientific pursuits, and who have signally failed in gaining recognition among their fellows, are endeavoring to make reputations among the churches by delivering weak and vapid lectures upon the "harmony of Genesis and Geology." Like all hypocrites, these men overstate the case to such a degree, and so turn and pervert facts and words that they succeed only in gaining the applause of other hypocrites like themselves. Among the great scientists they are regarded as generals regard sutlers who trade with both armies.

Surely the time must come when the wealth of the world will not be wasted in the propagation of ignorant creeds and miraculous mistakes. The time must come when churches and cathedrals will be dedicated to the use of man; when minister and priest will deem the discoveries of the living of more importance than the errors of the dead; when the truths of Nature will outrank the "sacred" falsehoods of the past, and when a single fact will outweigh all the miracles of Holy Writ.

Who car over estimate the progress of the world if all the money wasted in superstition could be used to enlighten, elevate and civilize mankind?

When every church becomes a school, every cathedral a university, every clergyman a teacher, and all their hearers brave and honest thinkers, then, and not until then, will the dream of poet, patriot, philanthropist and philosopher, become a real and blessed truth.

III.

THE POLITICIANS.

I WOULD like also to liberate the politician. At present, the successful office-seeker is a good deal like the centre of the earth ; he weighs nothing himself, but draws everything else to him. There are so many societies, so many churches, so many isms, that it is almost impossible for an independent man to succeed in a political career. Candidates are forced to pretend that they are Catholics with Protestant proclivities, or Christians with liberal tendencies, or temperance men who now and then take a glass of wine, or, that although not members of any church their wives are, and that they subscribe liberally to all. The result of all this is that we reward hypocrisy and elect men entirely destitute of real principle ; and this will never change until the people become grand enough to allow each other to do their own thinking.

Our Government should be entirely and purely secular. The religious views of a candidate should be kept entirely out of sight. He should not be compelled to give his opinion as to the inspiration of the Bible, the propriety of infant baptism, or the immaculate conception. All these things are private and personal. He should be allowed to settle such things for himself, and should he decide contrary to the law and will of God, let him settle the matter with God. The people ought to be wise enough to select as their officers men who know something of political affairs, who comprehend the present greatness, and clearly perceive the future grandeur of our country. If we were in a storm at sea, with deck wave-washed and masts strained and bent with storm, and it was necessary to reef the top sail, we certainly would not ask the brave sailor who volunteered to go aloft, what his opinion was on the five points of Calvinism. Our Government has nothing to do with religion. It is neither Christian nor pagan; it is secular. But as long as the people persist in voting for or against men on account of their religious views, just so long will hypocrisy hold place and power. Just so long will the candidates crawl in the dust—hide their opinions, flatter those with whom they differ, pretend to agree with those whom they despise ; and just so long will honest men be trampled under foot. Churches are becoming political organizations. Nearly every Catholic is a Democrat ; nearly every Methodist in the North is a Republican.

It probably will not be long until the churches will divide as sharply upon political, as upon theological questions ; and when that day comes, if there are not liberals enough to hold the balance of power, this Government will be destroyed. The liberty of man is not safe in the hands of any church. Wherever the Bible and sword are in partnership, man is a slave.

All laws for the purpose of making man worship God, are born of the same spirit that kindled the fires of the *auto da fe*, and lovingly built the dungeons of the Inquisition. All laws defining and punishing blasphemy—making it a crime to give your honest ideas about the Bible, or to laugh at the ignorance of the ancient Jews, or to enjoy yourself on the Sabbath, or to give your opinion of Jehovah were passed by impudent bigots, and should be at once repealed by honest men. An infinite God ought to be able to protect himself, without going in

partnership with State Legislatures. Certainly he
ought not so to act that laws become necessary to
keep him from being laughed at. No one thinks
of protecting Shakespeare from ridicule, by the
threat of fine and imprisonment. It strikes me that
God might write a book that would not necessarily
excite the laughter of his children. In fact, I think
it would be safe to say that a real God could produce
a work that would excite the admiration of mankind.
Surely politicians could be better employed than in
passing laws to protect the literary reputation of the
Jewish God.

IV.

MAN AND WOMAN.

L ET us forget that we are Baptists, Methodists, Catholics, Presbyterians, or Freethinkers, and remember only that we are men and women. **After** all, *man* and *woman* are the highest possible titles. All other names belittle us, and show that we have, to a certain extent, given up our individuality, and have consented to wear the collar of authority—that we are followers. Throwing away these names, let us examine these questions not as partisans, but as human beings with hopes and fears in common.

We know that our opinions depend, to a great degree, upon our surroundings—upon race, country, and education. We are all the result of numberless conditions, and inherit vices and virtues, truths and prejudices. If we had been born in England, sur-rounded by wealth and clothed with power, most of

us would have been Episcopalians, and believed in
church and state.   We should have insisted that the
people needed a religion, and that not having
intellect enough to provide one for themselves, it
was our duty to make one for them, and then compel them to support it.   We should have believed it
indecent to officiate in a pulpit without wearing a
gown, and that prayers should be read from a book.
Had we belonged to the lower classes, we might have
been dissenters and protested against the mummeries
of the High Church.   Had we been born in Turkey,
most of us would have been Mohammedans and
believed in the inspiration of the Koran.   We should
have believed that Mohammed actually visited
heaven and became acquainted with an angel by the
name of Gabriel, who was so broad between the eyes
that it required three hundred days for a very
smart camel to travel the distance.   If some man
had denied this story we should probably have
denounced him as a dangerous person, one who was
endeavoring to undermine the foundations of society,
and to destroy all distinction between virtue and vice.
We should have said to him, "What do you propose
to give us in place of that angel?   We cannot afford
to give up an angel of that size for nothing."   We

would have insisted that the best and wisest men believed the Koran. We would have quoted from the works and letters of philosophers, generals and sultans, to show that the Koran was the best of books, and that Turkey was indebted to that book and to that alone for its greatness and prosperity. We would have asked that man whether he knew more than all the great minds of his country, whether he was so much wiser than his fathers? We would have pointed out to him the fact that thousands had been consoled in the hour of death by passages from the Koran; that they had died with glazed eyes brightened by visions of the heavenly harem, and gladly left this world of grief and tears. We would have regarded Christians as the vilest of men, and on all occasions would have repeated "There is but one God, and Mohammed is his prophet!"

So, if we had been born in India, we should in all probability have believed in the religion of that country. We should have regarded the old records as true and sacred, and looked upon a wandering priest as better than the men from whom he begged, and by whose labor he lived. We should have believed in a god with three heads instead of three gods with one head, as we do now.

Now and then some one says that the religion of his father and mother is good enough for him, and wonders why anybody should desire a better. Surely we are not bound to follow our parents in religion any more than in politics, science or art. China has been petrified by the worship of ancestors. If our parents had been satisfied with the religion of theirs, we would be still less advanced than we are. If we are, in any way, bound by the belief of our fathers, the doctrine will hold good back to the first people who had a religion; and if this doctrine is true, we ought now to be believers in that first religion. In other words, we would all be barbarians. You cannot show real respect to your parents by perpetuating their errors. Good fathers and mothers wish their children to advance, to overcome obstacles which baffled them, and to correct the errors of their education. If you wish to reflect credit upon your parents, accomplish more than they did, solve problems that they could not understand, and build better than they knew. To sacrifice your manhood upon the grave of your father is an honor to neither. Why should a son who has examined a subject, throw away his reason and adopt the views of his mother? Is not such a course dishonorable to both?

We must remember that this "ancestor" argument is as old at least as the second generation of men, that it has served no purpose except to enslave mankind, and results mostly from the fact that acquiescence is easier than investigation. This argument pushed to its logical conclusion, would prevent the advance of all people whose parents were not Freethinkers.

It is hard for many people to give up the religion in which they were born; to admit that their fathers were utterly mistaken, and that the sacred records of their country are but collections of myths and fables.

But when we look for a moment at the world, we find that each nation has its "sacred records"—its religion, and its ideas of worship. Certainly all cannot be right; and as it would require a life time to investigate the claims of these various systems, it is hardly fair to damn a man forever, simply because he happens to believe the wrong one. All these religions were produced by barbarians. Civilized nations have contented themselves with changing the religions of their barbaric ancestors, but they have made none. Nearly all these religions are intensely selfish. Each one was made by some contemptible little nation that regarded itself as of almost infinite importance, and looked upon the other nations as beneath the notice of their god. In all these countries it was a crime to deny the sacred records, to laugh at the priests, to speak disrespectfully of the gods, to fail to divide your substance with the lazy hypocrites who managed your affairs in the next world upon condition that you would support them in this. In the olden time these theological people who quartered themselves upon the honest and industrious, were called soothsayers, seers, charmers, prophets, enchanters, sorcerers, wizards, astrologers, and impostors, but now, they are known as clergymen.

We are no exception to the general rule, and consequently have our sacred books as well as the rest. Of course, it is claimed by many of our people that our books are the only true ones, the only ones that the real God ever wrote, or had anything whatever to do with. They insist that all other sacred books were written by hypocrites and impostors; that the Jews were the only people that God ever had any personal intercourse with, and that all other prophets and seers were inspired only by impudence and mendacity. True, it seems somewhat

strange that God should have chosen a barbarous
and unknown people who had little or nothing to do
with the other nations of the earth, as his messengers
to the rest of mankind.

It is not easy to account for an infinite God
making people so low in the scale of intellect as
to require a revelation. Neither is it easy to perceive why, if a revelation was necessary for all,
it was made only to a few. Of course, I know that it
is extremely wicked to suggest these thoughts, and
that ignorance is the only armor that can effectually
protect you from the wrath of God. I am aware
that investigators with all their genius, never find
the road to heaven ; that those who look where
they are going are sure to miss it, and that only
those who voluntarily put out their eyes and
implicitly depend upon blindness can surely keep the
narrow path.

Whoever reads our sacred book is compelled to
believe it or suffer forever the torments of the lost.
We are told that we have the privilege of examining
it for ourselves ; but this privilege is only extended
to us on the condition that we believe it whether it
appears reasonable or not. We may disagree with
others as much as we please upon the meaning of

all passages in the Bible, but we must not deny the truth of a single word. We must believe that the book is inspired. If we obey its every precept without believing in its inspiration we will be damned just as certainly as though we disobeyed its every word. We have no right to weigh it in the scales of reason—to test it by the laws of nature, or the facts of observation and experience. To do this, we are told, is to put ourselves above the word of God, and sit in judgment on the works of our creator.

For my part, I cannot admit that belief is a voluntary thing. It seems to me that evidence, even in spite of ourselves, will have its weight, and that whatever our wish may be, we are compelled to stand with fairness by the scales, and give the exact result. It will not do to say that we reject the Bible because we are wicked. Our wickedness must be ascertained not from our belief but from our acts.

I am told by the clergy that I ought not to attack the Bible ; that I am leading thousands to perdition and rendering certain the damnation of my own soul. They have had the kindness to advise me that, if my object is to make converts, I am pursuing the wrong course. They tell me to use gentler expressions, and more cunning words. Do they really wish me to make more converts? If their advice is honest, they are traitors to their trust. If their advice is not honest, then they are unfair with me. Certainly they should wish me to pursue the course that will make the fewest converts, and yet they pretend to tell me how my influence could be increased. It may be, that upon this principle John Bright advises America to adopt free trade, so that our country can become a successful rival of Great Britain. Sometimes I think that even ministers are not entirely candid.

Notwithstanding the advice of the clergy, I have concluded to pursue my own course, to tell my honest thoughts, and to have my freedom in this world whatever my fate may be in the next.

The real oppressor, enslaver and corrupter of the people is the Bible. That book is the chain that binds, the dungeon that holds the clergy. That book spreads the pall of superstition over the colleges and schools. That book puts out the eyes of science, and makes honest investigation a crime. That book unmans the politician and degrades the people. That book fills the world with bigotry, hypocrisy and fear. It plays the same part in our country that has been played by "sacred records" in all the nations of the world.

A little while ago I saw one of the Bibles of the Middle Ages. It was about two feet in length, and one and a half in width. It had immense oaken covers, with hasps, and clasps, and hinges large enough almost for the doors of a penitentiary. It was covered with pictures of winged angels and aureoled saints. In my imagination I saw this book carried to the cathedral altar in solemn pomp—heard the chant of robed and kneeling priests, felt the strange tremor of the organ's peal; saw the colored light streaming through windows stained and touched by blood and flame—the swinging censer with its perfumed incense rising to the mighty roof, dim with height and rich with legend carved in stone, while on the walls was hung, written in light, and shade, and all the colors that can tell of joy and tears, the pictured history of the martyred Christ. The people fell upon their knees. The book was opened, and the priest read the messages from God to man. To the multitude, the book itself was evidence enough that it was not the work of human hands. How could those little marks and lines and dots contain, like tombs, the thoughts of men, and how could they, touched by a ray of light from human eyes, give up their dead? How could these characters span the vast chasm dividing the present from the past, and make it possible for the living still to hear the voices of the dead?

V

THE PENTATEUCH.

THE first five books in our Bible are known as the Pentateuch. For a long time it was supposed that Moses was the author, and among the ignorant the supposition still prevails. As a matter of fact, it seems to be well settled that Moses had nothing to do with these books, and that they were not written until he had been dust and ashes for hundreds of years. But, as all the churches still insist that he was the author, that he wrote even an account of his own death and burial, let us speak of him as though these books were in fact written by him. As the Christians maintain that God was the real author, it makes but little difference whom he employed as his pen, or clerk.

Nearly all authors of sacred books have given an account of the creation of the universe, the origin of matter, and the destiny of the human race. Nearly

all have pointed out the obligation that man is under
to his creator for having placed him upon the earth,
and allowed him to live and suffer, and have taught
that nothing short of the most abject worship could
possibly compensate God for his trouble and labor
suffered and done for the good of man. They have
nearly all insisted that we should thank God for all
that is good in life; but they have not all informed
us as to whom we should hold responsible for the
evils we endure.

Moses differed from most of the makers of sacred
books by his failure to say anything of a future life,
by failing to promise heaven, and to threaten hell.
Upon the subject of a future state, there is not one
word in the Pentateuch. Probably at that early day
God did not deem it important to make a revelation
as to the eternal destiny of man. He seems to have
thought that he could control the Jews, at least, by
rewards and punishments in this world, and so he
kept the frightful realities of eternal joy and torment
a profound secret from the people of his choice. He
thought it far more important to tell the Jews their
origin than to enlighten them as to their destiny.

We must remember that every tribe and nation
has some way in which, the more striking phenomena

of nature are accounted for. These accounts are handed down by tradition, changed by numberless narrators as intelligence increases, or to account for newly discovered facts, or for the purpose of satisfying the appetite for the marvelous.

The way in which a tribe or nation accounts for day and night, the change of seasons, the fall of snow and rain, the flight of birds, the origin of the rainbow, the peculiarities of animals, the dreams of sleep, the visions of the insane, the existence of earthquakes, volcanoes, storms, lightning and the thousand things that attract the attention and excite the wonder, fear or admiration of mankind, may be called the philosophy of that tribe or nation. And as all phenomena are, by savage and barbaric man accounted for as the action of intelligent beings for the accomplishment of certain objects, and as these beings were supposed to have the power to assist or injure man, certain things were supposed necessary for man to do in order to gain the assistance, and avoid the anger of these gods. Out of this belief grew certain ceremonies, and these ceremonies united with the belief, formed religion; and consequently every religion has for its foundation a misconception of the cause of phenomena.

All worship is necessarily based upon the belief that some being exists who can, if he will, change the natural order of events. The savage prays to a stone that he calls a god, while the Christian prays to a god that he calls a spirit, and the prayers of both are equally useful. The savage and the Christian put behind the Universe an intelligent cause, and this cause whether represented by one god or many, has been, in all ages, the object of all worship. To carry a fetich, to utter a prayer, to count beads, to abstain from food, to sacrifice a lamb, a child or an enemy, are simply different ways by which the accomplishment of the same object is sought, and are all the offspring of the same error.

Many systems of religion must have existed many ages before the art of writing was discovered, and must have passed through many changes before the stories, miracles, histories, prophecies and mistakes became fixed and petrified in written words. After that, change was possible only by giving new meanings to old words, a process rendered necessary by the continual acquisition of facts somewhat inconsistent with a literal interpretation of the " sacred records." In this way an honest faith often prolongs

its life by dishonest methods ; and in this way he
Christians of to-day are trying to harmonize the
Mosaic account of creation with the theories and
discoveries of modern science.

Admitting that Moses was the author of the
Pentateuch, or that he gave to the Jews a religion,
the question arises as to where he obtained his information.   We are told by the theologians that he
received his knowledge from God, and that every
word he wrote was and is the exact truth.   It is
admitted at the same time that he was an adopted
son of Pharaoh's daughter, and enjoyed the rank and
privilege of a prince.   Under such circumstances, he
must have been well acquainted with the literature,
philosophy and religion of the Egyptians, and must
have known what they believed and taught as to the
creation of the world.

Now, if the account of the origin of this earth as
given by Moses is substantially like that given by
the Egyptians, then we must conclude that he learned
it from them.   Should we imagine that he was
divinely inspired because he gave to the Jews what
the Egyptians had given him ?

The Egyptian priests taught *first*, that a god
created the original matter, leaving it in a state of

chaos ; *second*, that a god moulded it into form; *third*, that the breath of a god moved upon the face of the deep; *fourth*, that a god created simply by saying "Let it be;" *fifth*, that a god created light before the sun existed.

Nothing can be clearer than that Moses received from the Egyptians the principal parts of his narrative, making such changes and additions as were necessary to satisfy the peculiar superstitions of his own people.

If some man at the present day should assert that he had received from God the theories of evolution, the survival of the fittest, and the law of heredity, and we should afterwards find that he was not only an Englishman, but had lived in the family of Charles Darwin, we certainly would account for his having these theories in a natural way,   So, if Darwin himself should pretend that he was inspired, and had obtained his peculiar theories from God, we should probably reply that his grandfather suggested the same ideas, and that Lamarck published substantially the same theories the same year that Mr. Darwin was born.

Now, if we have sufficient courage, we will, by the same course of reasoning, account for the story

of creation found in the Bible. We will say that
it contains the belief of Moses, and that he received
his information from the Egyptians, and not from
God. If we take the account as the absolute truth
and use it for the purpose of determining the value
of modern thought, scientific advancement becomes
impossible. And even if the account of the creation
as given by Moses should turn out to be true, and
should be so admitted by all the scientific world, the
claim that he was inspired would still be without the
least particle of proof. We would be forced to admit
that he knew more than we had supposed. It certainly is no proof that a man is inspired simply
because he is right.

No one pretends that Shakespeare was inspired,
and yet all the writers of the books of the Old Testament put together, could not have produced
Hamlet.

Why should we, looking upon some rough and
awkward thing, or god in stone, say that it must have
been produced by some inspired sculptor, and with the
same breath pronounce the *Venus de Milo* to be the
work of man? Why should we, looking at some
ancient daub of angel, saint or virgin, say its painter
must have been assisted by a god?

Let us account for all we see by the facts we know. If there are things for which we cannot account, let us wait for light. To account for anything by supernatural agencies is, in fact to say that we do not know. Theology is not what we know about God, but what we do not know about Nature. In order to increase our respect for the Bible, it became necessary for the priests to exalt and extol that book, and at the same time to decry and belittle the reasoning powers of man. The whole power of the pulpit has been used for hundreds of years to destroy the confidence of man in himself—to induce him to distrust his own powers of thought, to believe that he was wholly unable to decide any question for himself, and that all human virtue consists in faith and obedience. The church has said, " Believe, and obey! If you reason, you will become an unbeliever, and unbelievers will be lost. If you disobey, you will do so through vain pride and curiosity, and will, like Adam and Eve, be thrust from Paradise forever ! "

For my part, I care nothing for what the church says, except in so far as it accords with my reason ; and the Bible is nothing to me, only in so far as it agrees with what I think or know.

All books should be examined in the same spirit, and truth should be welcomed and falsehood exposed, no matter in what volume they may be found.

Let us in this spirit examine the Peutateuch; and if anything appears unreasonable, contradictory or absurd, let us have the honesty and courage to admit it. Certainly no good can result either from deceiving ourselves or others. Many millions have implicitly believed this book, and have just as implicitly believed that polygamy was sanctioned by God. Millions have regarded this book as the foundation of all human progress, and at the same time looked upon slavery as a divine institution. Millions have declared this book to have been infinitely holy, and to prove that they were right, have imprisoned, robbed and burned their fellow-men. The inspiration of this book has been established by famine, sword and fire, by dungeon, chain and whip, by dagger and by rack, by force and fear and fraud, and generations have been frightened by threats of hell, and bribed with promises of heaven.

Let us examine a portion of this book, not in the darkness of our fear, but in the light of reason.

And first, let us examine the account given of the creation of this world, commenced, according to the Bible, on Monday morning about five thousand eight hundred and eighty-three years ago.

VI.

MONDAY.

MOSES commences his story by telling us that in the beginning God created the heaven and the earth.

If this means anything, it means that God produced, caused to exist, called into being, the heaven and the earth. It will not do to say that he formed the heaven and the earth of previously existing matter. Moses conveys, and intended to convey the idea that the matter of which the heaven and the earth are composed, was created.

It is impossible for me to conceive of something being created from nothing. Nothing, regarded in the light of a raw material, is a decided failure. I cannot conceive of matter apart from force. Neither is it possible to think of force disconnected with matter. You cannot imagine matter going back to absolute nothing. Neither can you imagine nothing being changed into something. You may be eternally damned if you do not say that you can conceive these things, but you cannot conceive them.

Such is the constitution of the human mind that it cannot even think of a commencement or an end of matter, or force.

If God created the universe, there was a time when he commenced to create. Back of that commencement there must have been an eternity. In that eternity what was this God doing? He certainly did not think. There was nothing to think about. He did not remember. Nothing had ever happened. What did he do? Can you imagine anything more absurd than an infinite intelligence in infinite nothing wasting an eternity?

I do not pretend to tell how all these things really are; but I do insist that a statement that cannot possibly be comprehended by any human being, and that appears utterly impossible, repugnant to every fact of experience, and contrary to everything that we really know, must be rejected by every honest man.

We can conceive of eternity, because we cannot conceive of a cessation of time. We can conceive of infinite space because we cannot conceive of so much matter that our imagination will not stand upon the farthest star, and see infinite space beyond. In other words, we cannot conceive of a cessation of time;

therefore eternity is a necessity of the mind.
Eternity sustains the same relation to time that space
does to matter.

In the time of Moses, it was perfectly safe for him
to write an account of the creation of the world. He
had simply to put in form the crude notions of the
people. At that time, no other Jew could have
written a better account. Upon that subject he felt
at liberty to give his imagination full play. There
was no one who could authoritatively contradict any
thing he might say. It was substantially the same
story that had been imprinted in curious characters
upon the clay records of Babylon, the gigantic
monuments of Egypt, and the gloomy temples of
India. In those days there was an almost infinite
difference between the educated and ignorant. The
people were controlled almost entirely by signs and
wonders. By the lever of fear, priests moved the
world. The sacred records were made and kept,
and altered by them. The people could not read,
and looked upon one who could, as almost a god.
In our day it is hard to conceive of the influence of
an educated class in a barbarous age. It was only
necessary to produce the "sacred record," and
ignorance fell upon its face. The people were taught

that the record was inspired, and therefore true. They were not taught that it was true, and therefore inspired.

After all, the real question is not whether the Bible is inspired, but whether it is true. If it is true, it does not need to be inspired. If it is true, it makes no difference whether it was written by a man or a god. The multiplication table is just as useful, just as true as though God had arranged the figures himself. If the Bible is really true, the claim of inspiration need not be urged; and if it is not true, its inspiration can hardly be established. As a matter of fact, the truth does not need to be inspired. Nothing needs inspiration except a falsehood or a mistake. Where truth ends, where probability stops, inspiration begins. A fact never went into partnership with a miracle. Truth does not need the assistance of miracle. A fact will fit every other fact in the Universe, because it is the product of all other facts. A lie will fit nothing except another lie made for the express purpose of fitting it. After a while the man gets tired of lying, and then the last lie will not fit the next fact, and then there is an opportunity to use a miracle. Just at that point, it is necessary to have a little inspiration.

It seems to me that reason is the highest attribute of man, and that if there can be any communication from God to man, it must be addressed to his reason. It does not seem possible that in order to understand a message from God it is absolutely essential to throw our reason away. How could God make known his will to any being destitute of reason? How can any man accept as a revelation from God that which is unreasonable to him? God cannot make a revelation to another man for me. He must make it to me, and until he convinces my reason that it is true, I cannot receive it.

The statement that in the beginning God created the heaven and the earth, I cannot accept. It is contrary to my reason, and I cannot believe it. It appears reasonable to me that force has existed from eternity. Force cannot, as it appears to me, exist apart from matter. Force, in its nature, is forever active, and without matter it could not act; and so I think matter must have existed forever. To conceive of matter without force, or of force without matter, or of a time when neither existed, or of a being who existed for an eternity without either, and who out of nothing created both, is to me utterly impossible. I may be damned on this account, but I cannot help it. In my judgment, Moses was mistaken.

It will not do to say that Moses merely intended to tell what God did, in making the heavens and the earth out of matter then in existence. He distinctly states that in the *beginning* God created them. If this account is true, we must believe that God, existing in infinite space surrounded by eternal nothing, naught and void, created, produced, called into being, willed into existence this universe of countless stars.

The next thing we are told by this inspired gentleman is, that God created light, and proceeded to divide it from the darkness.

Certainly, the person who wrote this believed that darkness was a thing, an entity, a material that could get mixed and tangled up with light, and that these entities, light and darkness, had to be separated. In his imagination he probably saw God throwing pieces and chunks of darkness on one side, and rays and beams of light on the other. It is hard for a man who has been born but once to understand these things. For my part, I cannot understand how light can be separated from darkness. I had always supposed that darkness was simply the absence of light, and that under no circumstances could it be necessary to take the darkness away from the light. It is certain, however, that Moses believed darkness to be a form of matter, because I find that in another place he speaks of a darkness that could be felt. They used to have on exhibition at Rome a bottle of the darkness that overspread Egypt.

You cannot divide light from darkness any more than you can divide heat from cold. Cold is an absence of heat, and darkness is an absence of light. I suppose that we have no conception of absolute cold. We know only degrees of heat. Twenty degrees below zero is just twenty degrees warmer than forty degrees below zero. Neither cold nor darkness are entities, and these words express simply either the absolute or partial absence of heat or light. I cannot conceive how light can be divided from darkness, but I can conceive how a barbarian several thousand years ago, writing upon a subject about which he knew nothing, could make a mistake. The creator of light could not have written in this way. If such a being exists, he must have known the nature of that " mode of motion " that paints the earth on every eye, and clothes in garments seven-hued this universe of worlds.

VII.

TUESDAY.

WE are next informed by Moses that "God said Let there be a firmament in the midst of the waters, and let it divide the waters from the waters;" and that "God made the firmament, and divided the waters which were under the firmament from the waters which were above the firmament."

What did the writer mean by the word firmament? Theologians now tell us that he meant an "expanse." This will not do. How could an expanse divide the waters from the waters, so that the waters above the expanse would not fall into and mingle with the waters below the expanse? The truth is that Moses regarded the firmament as a solid affair. It was where God lived, and where water was kept. It was for this reason that they used to pray for rain. They supposed that some angel could with a lever raise a gate and let out the quantity of moisture desired. It was with the water from this firmament that the world was drowned when the windows of heaven were opened. It was in this

firmament that the sons of God lived—the sons who
" saw the daughters of men that they were fair and
took them wives of all which they chose." The
issue of such marriages were giants, and " the same
became mighty men which were of old, men of
renown."

Nothing is clearer than that Moses regarded the
firmament as a vast material division that separated
the waters of the world, and upon whose floor God
lived, surrounded by his sons. In no other way could
he account for rain. Where did the water come
from? He knew nothing about the laws of evapo-
ration. He did not know that the sun wooed with
amorous kisses the waves of the sea, and that they,
clad in glorified mist rising to meet their lover, were,
by disappointment, changed to tears and fell as
rain.

The idea that the firmament was the abode of
the Deity must have been in the mind of Moses
when he related the dream of Jacob. " And he
dreamed, and behold, a ladder set upon the earth
and the top of it reached to heaven ; and behold the
angels of God ascending and descending on it ; and
behold the Lord stood above it and said, I am the
Lord God."

So, when the people were building the tower of Babel "the Lord came down to see the city, and the tower which the children of men builded. And the Lord said, Behold the people is one, and they have all one language : and this they begin to do ; and nothing will be restrained from them which they imagined to do. Go to, let us go down and confound their language that they may not understand one another's speech."

The man who wrote that absurd account must have believed that God lived above the earth, in the firmament. The same idea was in the mind of the Psalmist when he said that God "bowed the heavens and came down."

Of course, God could easily remove any person bodily to heaven, as it was but a little way above the earth. "Enoch walked with God, and he was not, for God took him." The accounts in the Bible of the ascension of Elijah, Christ and St. Paul were born of the belief that the firmament was the dwelling-place of God. It probably never occurred to these writers that if the firmament was seven or eight miles away, Enoch and the rest would have been frozen perfectly stiff long before the journey could have been completed. Possibly Elijah might have made the voyage, as he was carried to heaven in a chariot of fire "by a whirlwind."

The truth is, that Moses was mistaken, and upon that mistake the Christians located their heaven and their hell. The telescope destroyed the firmament, did away with the heaven of the New Testament, rendered the ascension of our Lord and the assumption of his Mother infinitely absurd, crumbled to chaos the gates and palaces of the New Jerusalem, and in their places gave to man a wilderness of worlds.

VIII.

WEDNESDAY.

WE are next informed by the historian of creation, that after God had finished making the firmament and had succeeded in dividing the waters by means of an "expanse," he proceeded "to gather the waters on the earth together in seas, so that the dry land might appear."

Certainly the writer of this did not have any conception of the real form of the earth. He could not have known anything of the attraction of gravitation. He must have regarded the earth as flat and supposed that it required considerable force and power to induce the water to leave the mountains and collect in the valleys. Just as soon as the water was forced to run down hill, the dry land appeared, and the grass began to grow, and the mantles of green were thrown over the shoulders of the hills, and the trees laughed into bud and blossom, and the branches were laden with fruit. And all this happened before a ray had left the quiver of the sun, before a glittering beam had thrilled the bosom of a flower, and before the Dawn with trembling hands had drawn aside the curtains of the East and welcomed to her arms the eager god of Day.

It does not seem to me that grass and trees could grow and ripen into seed and fruit without the sun. According to the account, this all happened on the third day.   Now, if, as the Christians say, Moses did not mean by the word day a period of twenty-four hours, but an immense and almost measureless space of time, and as God did not, according to this view make any animals until the fifth day, that is, not for millions of years after he made the grass and trees, for what purpose did he cause the trees to bear fruit?

Moses says that God said on the third day, "Let the earth bring forth grass, the herb yielding seed, and the fruit tree yielding fruit after his kind, whose seed is in itself upon the earth; and it was so.   And the earth brought forth grass and herb yielding seed after his kind, and the tree yielding fruit whose seed was in itself after his kind; and God saw that it was good, and the evening and the morning were the third day."

There was nothing to eat this fruit; not an insect with painted wings sought the honey of the flowers;

not a single living, breathing thing upon the earth. Plenty of grass, a great variety of herbs, an abundance of fruit, but not a mouth in all the world.   If Moses is right, this state of things lasted only two days; but if the modern theologians are correct, it continued for millions of ages.

"It is now well known that the organic history of the earth can be properly divided into five epochs— the Primordial, Primary, Secondary, Tertiary, and Quaternary.   Each of these epochs is characterized by animal and vegetable life peculiar to itself.   In the First will be found Algæ and Skull-less Vertebrates, in the Second, Ferns and Fishes, in the Third, Pine Forests and Reptiles, in the Fourth, Foliaceous Forests and Mammals, and in the Fifth, Man."

How much more reasonable this is than the idea that the earth was covered with grass, and herbs, and trees loaded with fruit for millions of years before an animal existed.

There is, in Nature, an even balance forever kept between the total amounts of animal and vegetable life.   "In her wonderful economy she must form and bountifully nourish her vegetable progeny—twin-brother life to her, with that of animals.   The perfect balance between plant existences and animal existences must always be maintained, while matter courses through the eternal circle, becoming each in turn. If an animal be resolved into its ultimate constituents in a period according to the surrounding circumstances, say, of four hours, of four months, of four years, or even of four thousand years,—for it is impossible to deny that there may be instances of all these periods during which the process has continued —those elements which assume the gaseous form mingle at once with the atmosphere and are taken up from it without delay by the ever-open mouths of vegetable life. By a thousand pores in every leaf the carbonic acid which renders the atmosphere unfit for animal life is absorbed, the carbon being separated, and assimilated to form the vegetable fibre, which, as wood, makes and furnishes our houses and ships, is burned for our warmth, or is stored up under pressure for coal. All this carbon has played its part, and many parts in its time, as animal existences from monad up to man. Our mahogany of to-day has been many negroes in its turn, and before the African existed, was integral portions of many a generation of extinct species."

It seems reasonable to suppose that certain kinds of vegetation and certain kinds of animals should exist together, and that as the character of the vegetation changed, a corresponding change would take place in the animal world. It may be that I am led to these conclusions by "total depravity," or that I lack the necessary humility of spirit to satisfactorily harmonize Haeckel and Moses ; or that I am carried away by pride, blinded by reason, given over to hardness of heart that I might be damned, but I never can believe that the earth was covered with leaves, and buds, and flowers, and fruits before the sun with glittering spear had driven back the hosts of Night.

IX.

THURSDAY.

AFTER the world was covered with vegetation, it occurred to Moses that it was about time to make a sun and moon; and so we are told that on the fourth day God said, "Let there be light in the firmament of the heaven to divide the day from the night; and let them be for signs and for seasons, and for days and years ; and let them be for lights in the firmament of the heaven to give light upon the earth ; and it was so.   And God made two great lights ; the greater light to rule the day, and the lesser light to rule the night; he made the stars also."

Can we believe that the inspired writer had any idea of the size of the sun ? Draw a circle five inches in diameter, and by its side thrust a pin through the paper.   The hole made by the pin will sustain about the same relation to the circle that the earth does to the sun.   Did he know that the sun was eight hundred and sixty thousand miles in diameter ; that it was enveloped in an ocean of fire thousands of miles in depth, hotter even than the Christian's hell, over which sweep tempests of flame moving at the rate of one hundred miles a second, compared with which the wildest storm that ever wrecked the forests of this world was but a calm? Did he know that the sun every moment of time throws out as much heat as could be generated by the combustion of millions upon millions of tons of coal? Did he know that the volume of the earth is less than one-millionth of that of the sun? Did he know of the one hundred and four planets belonging to our solar system, all children of the sun? Did he know of Jupiter eighty-five thousand miles in diameter, hundreds of times as large as our earth, turning on his axis at the rate of twenty-five thousand miles an hour accompanied by four moons, making the tour of his orbit in fifty years, a distance of three thousand million miles? Did he know anything about Saturn, his rings and his eight moons? Did he have the faintest idea that all these planets were once a part of the sun; that the vast luminary was once thousands of millions of miles in diameter; that Neptune, Uranus, Saturn, Jupiter and Mars were all born before our earth, and that by no possibility could this world have existed three days, nor three periods, nor three " good whiles " before its source, the sun?

Moses supposed the sun to be about three or four feet in diameter and the moon about half that size. Compared with the earth they were but simple specks. This idea seems to have been shared by all the "inspired" men. We find in the book of Joshua that the sun stood still, and the moon stayed until the people had avenged themselves upon their enemies. "So the sun stood still in the midst of heaven, and hasted not to go down about a whole day."

We are told that the sacred writer wrote in common speech as we do when we talk about the rising and setting of the sun, and that all he intended to say was that the earth ceased to turn on its axis "for about a whole day."

My own opinion is that General Joshua knew no more about the motions of the earth than he did about mercy and justice. If he had known that the earth turned upon its axis at the rate of a thousand miles an hour, and swept in its course about the sun at the rate of sixty-eight thousand miles an hour, he would have doubled the hailstones, spoken of in the same chapter, that the Lord cast down from heaven, and allowed the sun and moon to rise and set in the usual way.

It is impossible to conceive of a more absurd story than this about the stopping of the sun and moon, and yet nothing so excites the malice of the orthodox preacher as to call its truth in question. Some endeavor to account for the phenomenon by natural causes, while others attempt to show that God could, by the refraction of light have made the sun visible although actually shining on the opposite side of the earth. The last hypothesis has been seriously urged by ministers within the last few months. The Rev. Henry M. Morey of South Bend, Indiana, says "that the phenomenon was simply optical. The rotary motion of the earth was not disturbed, but the light of the sun was prolonged by the same laws of refraction and reflection by which the sun now appears to be above the horizon when it is really below. The medium through which the sun's rays passed may have been miraculously influenced so as to have caused the sun to linger above the horizon long after its usual time for disappearance."

This is the latest and ripest product of Christian scholarship upon this question no doubt, but still it is not entirely satisfactory to me. According to the sacred account the sun did not linger, merely, above the horizon, but stood still "in the midst of heaven for about a whole day," that is to say, for about twelve hours. If the air was miraculously changed, so that it would refract the rays of the sun while the earth turned over as usual for "about a whole day," then, at the end of that time the sun must have been visible in the east, that is, it must by that time have been the next morning. According to this, that most wonderful day must have been at least thirty-six hours in length. We have first, the twelve hours of natural light, then twelve hours of "refracted and reflected" light. By that time it would again be morning, and the sun would shine for twelve hours more in the natural way, making thirty-six hours in all.

If the Rev. Morey would depend a little less on "refraction" and a little more on "reflection," he would conclude that the whole story is simply a barbaric myth and fable.

It hardly seems reasonable that God, if there is one, would either stop the globe, change the constitution of the atmosphere or the nature of light simply to afford Joshua an opportunity to kill people on that day when he could just as easily have waited until the next morning. It certainly cannot be very gratifying to God for us to believe such childish things.

It has been demonstrated that force is eternal ; that it is forever active, and eludes destruction by change of form. Motion is a form of force, and all arrested motion changes instantly to heat. The earth turns upon its axis at about one thousand miles an hour. Let it be stopped and a force beyond our imagination is changed to heat. It has been calculated that to stop the world would produce as much heat as the burning of a solid piece of coal three times the size of the earth. And yet we are asked to believe that this was done in order that one barbarian might defeat another. Such stories never would have been written, had not the belief been general that the heavenly bodies were as nothing compared with the earth.

The view of Moses was acquiesced in by the Jewish people and by the Christian world for thousands of years. It is supposed that Moses lived about fifteen hundred years before Christ, and although he was "inspired," and obtained his information directly from God, he did not know as much about our solar system as the Chinese did a thousand years before he was born. "The Emperor Chwenhio adopted as an epoch, a conjunction of the planets Mercury, Mars, Jupiter and Saturn, which has been shown by M. Bailly to have occurred no less than 2449 years before Christ." The ancient Chinese knew not only the motions of the planets, but they could calculate eclipses. "In the reign of the Emperor Chow-Kang, the chief astronomers, Ho and Hi were condemned to death for neglecting to announce a solar eclipse which took place 2169 B. C., a clear proof that the prediction of eclipses was a part of the duty of the imperial astronomers."

Is it not strange that a Chinaman should find out by his own exertions more about the material universe than Moses could when assisted by its Creator?

About eight hundred years after God gave Moses the principal facts about the creation of the "heaven and the earth" he performed another miracle far more wonderful than stopping the world. On this occasion he not only stopped the earth, but actually caused it to turn the other way. A Jewish king was sick, and God, in order to convince him that he would ultimately recover, offered to make the shadow on the dial go forward, or backward ten degrees. The king thought it was too easy a thing to make the shadow go forward, and asked that it be turned back. Thereupon, "Isaiah the prophet cried unto the Lord, and he brought the shadow ten degrees backward by which it had gone down in the dial of Ahaz." I hardly see how this miracle could be accounted for even by " refraction " and " reflection."

It seems, from the account, that this stupendous miracle was performed after the king had been cured. The account of the shadow going backward is given in the eleventh verse of the twentieth chapter of Second Kings, while the cure is given in the seventh verse of the same chapter. " And Isaiah said, Take a lump of figs. And they took and laid it on the boil, and he recovered."

Stopping the world and causing it to turn back ten degrees after that, seems to have been, as the boil was already cured by the figs, a useless display of power.

The easiest way to account for all these wonders is to say that the "inspired" writers were mistaken. In this way a fearful burden is lifted from the credulity of man, and he is left free to believe the evidences of his own senses, and the demonstrations of science. In this way he can emancipate himself from the slavery of superstition, the control of the barbaric dead, and the despotism of the church.

Only about a hundred years ago, Buffon, the naturalist, was compelled by the faculty of theology at Paris to publicly renounce fourteen "errors" in his work on Natural History because they were at variance with the Mosaic account of creation. The Pentateuch is still the scientific standard of the church, and ignorant priests, armed with that, pronounce sentence upon the vast accomplishments of modern thought.

X

"HE MADE THE STARS ALSO."

Moses came very near forgetting about the stars and only gave five words to all the hosts of heaven. Can it be possible that he knew anything about the stars beyond the mere fact that he saw them shining above him?

Did he know that the nearest star, the one we ought to be the best acquainted with, is twenty-one billion of miles away, and that it is a sun shining by its own light? Did he know of the next, that is thirty-seven billion miles distant? Is it possible that he was acquainted with Sirius, a sun two thousand six hundred and eighty-eight times larger than our own, surrounded by a system of heavenly bodies, several of which are already known, and distant from us eighty-two billion miles? Did he know that the Polar star that tells the mariner his course and guided slaves to liberty and joy, is distant from this little world two hundred and ninety-two billion miles.

and that Capella wheels and shines one hundred and thirty-three billion miles beyond? Did he know that it would require about seventy-two years for light to reach us from this star? Did he know that light travels one hundred and eighty-five thousand miles a second? Did he know that some stars are so far away in the infinite abysses that five millions of years are required for their light to reach this globe?

If this is true, and if as the Bible tells us, the stars were made after the earth, then this world has been wheeling in its orbit for at least five million years.

It may be replied that it was not the intention of God to teach geology and astronomy. Then why did he say anything upon these subjects? and if he did say anything, why did he not give the facts?

According to the sacred records God created, on the first day, the heaven and the earth, "moved upon the face of the waters," and made the light. On the second day he made the firmament or the "expanse" and divided the waters. On the third day he gathered the waters into seas, let the dry land appear and caused the earth to bring forth grass, herbs and fruit trees, and on the fourth day he made the sun, moon and stars and set them in the firmament of heaven to give light upon the earth. This division of labor is very striking. The work of the other days is as nothing when compared with that of the fourth. Is it possible that it required the same time and labor to make the grass, herbs and fruit trees, that it did to fill with countless constellations the infinite expanse of space?

XI.

FRIDAY.

WE are then told that on the next day "God said, Let the waters bring forth abundantly the moving creatures that hath life, and fowl that may fly above the earth in the open firmament of heaven. And God created great whales and every living creature which the waters brought forth abundantly, after their kind, and every winged fowl after his kind, and God saw that it was good. And God blessed them, saying, Be fruitful and multiply and fill the waters in the seas, and let fowl multiply in the earth."

Is it true that while the dry land was covered with grass, and herbs, and trees bearing fruit, the ocean was absolutely devoid of life, and so remained for millions of years?

If Moses meant twenty-four hours by the word day, then it would make but little difference on which of the six days animals were made ; but if the word day was used to express millions of ages, during which life was slowly evolved from monad up to man, then the account becomes infinitely absurd, puerile and foolish. There is not a scientist of high standing who will say that in his judgment the earth was covered with fruit-bearing trees before the moners, the ancestors it may be of the human race, felt in Laurentian seas the first faint throb of life. Nor is there one who will declare that there was a single spire of grass before the sun had poured upon the world his flood of gold.

Why should men in the name of religion try to harmonize the contradictions that exist between Nature and a book? Why should philosophers be denounced for placing more reliance upon what they know than upon what they have been told? If there is a God, it is reasonably certain that he made the world, but it is by no means certain that he is the author of the Bible. Why then should we not place greater confidence in Nature than in a book? And even if this God made not only the world but the book besides, it does not follow that the book is the best part of creation, and the only part that we will be eternally punished for denying. It seems to me that it is quite as important to know something of the solar system, something of the physical history of this globe, as it is to know the adventures of Jonah or the diet of Ezekiel. For my part, I would infinitely prefer to know all the results of scientific investigation, than to be inspired as Moses was. Supposing the Bible to be true ; why is it any worse or more wicked for Freethinkers to deny it, than for priests to deny the doctrine of evolution, or the dynamic theory of heat ? Why should we be damned for laughing at Samson and his foxes, while others, holding the Nebular Hypothesis in utter contempt, go straight to heaven ? It seems to me that a belief in the great truths of science are fully as essential to salvation, as the creed of any church. We are taught that a man may be perfectly acceptable to God even if he denies the rotundity of the earth, the Copernican system, the three laws of Kepler, the indestructibility of matter and the attraction of gravitation. And we are also taught that a man may be right upon all these questions, and yet, for failing to believe in the " scheme of salvation," be eternally lost.

XII.

SATURDAY.

O N this, the last day of creation, God said:—
"Let the earth bring forth the living creature after his kind, cattle and creeping thing and beast of the earth after his kind; and it was so. And God made the beast of the earth after his kind, and cattle after their kind, and every thing that creepeth upon the earth after his kind; and God saw that it was good."

Now, is it true that the seas were filled with fish, the sky with fowls, and the earth covered with grass, and herbs, and fruit bearing trees, millions of ages before there was a creeping thing in existence? Must we admit that plants and animals were the result of the fiat of some incomprehensible intelligence independent of the operation of what are known as natural causes? Why is a miracle any more necessary to account for yesterday than for to-day or for to-morrow?

If there is an infinite Power, nothing can be more
certain than that this Power works in accordance with
what we call law, that is, by and through natural
causes.   If anything can be found without a pedigree
of natural antecedents, it will then be time enough to
talk about the fiat of creation.   There must have
been a time when plants and animals did not exist
upon this globe.   The question, and the only question
is, whether they were naturally produced.   If the
account given by Moses is true, then the vegetable
and animal existences are the result of certain special
fiats of creation entirely independent of the operation
of natural causes.   This is so grossly improbable, so at
variance with the experience and observation of mankind, that it cannot be adopted without abandoning
forever the basis of scientific thought and action.

It may be urged that we do not understand the
sacred record correctly.   To this it may be replied
that for thousands of years the account of the creation
has, by the Jewish and Christian world, been regarded
as literally true.   If it was inspired, of course God
must have known just how it would be understood,
and consequently must have intended that it should
be understood just as he knew it would be.   One
man writing to another, may mean one thing, and

yet be understood as meaning something else.
Now, if the writer knew that he would be misunder-
stood, and also knew that he could use other words
that would convey his real meaning, but did not, we
would say that he used words on purpose to mislead,
and was not an honest man.

If a being of infinite wisdom wrote the Bible, or
caused it to be written, he must have known exactly
how his words would be interpreted by all the world,
and he must have intended to convey the very
meaning that was conveyed. He must have known
that by reading that book, man would form erroneous
views as to the shape, antiquity, and size of this
world; that he would be misled as to the time and
order of creation; that he would have the most
childish and contemptible views of the creator; that
the "sacred word" would be used to support slavery
and polygamy; that it would build dungeons for the
good, and light fagots to consume the brave, and
therefore he must have intended that these results
should follow. He also must have known that
thousands and millions of men and women never
could believe his Bible, and that the number of unbelievers would increase in the exact ratio of civilization,
and therefore, he must have intended that result.

Let us understand this. An honest finite being uses the best words, in his judgment, to convey his meaning. This is the best he can do, because he cannot certainly know the exact effect of his words on others. But an infinite being must know not only the real meaning of the words, but the exact meaning they will convey to every reader and hearer. He must know every meaning that they are capable of conveying to every mind. He must also know what explanations must be made to prevent misconception. If an infinite being cannot, in making a revelation to man, use such words that every person to whom a revelation is essential will understand distinctly what that revelation is, then a revelation from God through the instrumentality of language is impossible, or it is not essential that all should understand it correctly. It may be urged that millions have not the capacity to understand a revelation, although expressed in the plainest words. To this it seems a sufficient reply to ask, why a being of infinite power should create men so devoid of intelligence, that he cannot by any means make known to them his will? We are told that it is exceedingly plain, and that a wayfaring man, though a fool, need not err therein. This statement is refuted by the religious history of the

Christian world.   Every sect is a certificate that God
has not plainly revealed his will to man.   To each
reader the Bible conveys a different meaning.   About
the meaning of this book, called a revelation, there
have been ages of war, and centuries of sword and
flame.   If written by an infinite God, he must have
known that these results must follow ; and thus
knowing, he must be responsible for all.

Is it not infinitely more reasonable to say that
this book is the work of man, that it is filled with
mingled truth and error, with mistakes and facts, and
reflects, too faithfully perhaps, the " very form and
pressure of its time " ?

If there are mistakes in the Bible, certainly they
were made by man.   If there is anything contrary to
nature, it was written by man.   If there is anything
immoral, cruel, heartless or infamous, it certainly was
never written by a being worthy of the adoration
of mankind.

XIII.

LET US MAKE MAN.

WE are next informed by the author of the Pentateuch that God said "Let us make man in our image, after our likeness," and that "God created man in his own image, in the image of God created he him—male and female created he them."

If this account means anything, it means that man was created in the physical image and likeness of God. Moses while he speaks of man as having been made in the image of God, never speaks of God except as having the form of a man. He speaks of God as "walking in the garden in the cool of the day;" and that Adam and Eve "heard his voice." He is constantly telling what God said, and in a thousand passages he refers to him as not only having the human form, but as performing actions, such as man performs. The God of Moses was a God with hands, with feet, with the organs of speech.

A God of passion, of hatred, of revenge, of affection, of repentance; a God who made mistakes:—in other words, an immense and powerful man.

It will not do to say that Moses meant to convey the idea that God made man in his mental or moral image. Some have insisted that man was made in the moral image of God because he was made pure. Purity cannot be manufactured. A moral character cannot be made for man by a god. Every man must make his own moral character. Consequently, if God is infinitely pure, Adam and Eve were not made in his image in that respect. Others say that Adam and Eve were made in the mental image of God. If it is meant by that, that they were created with reasoning powers like, but not to the extent of those possessed by a god, then this may be admitted. But certainly this idea was not in the mind of Moses. He regarded the human form as being in the image of God, and for that reason always spoke of God as having that form. No one can read the Pentateuch without coming to the conclusion that the author supposed that man was created in the physical likeness of Deity. God said " Go to, let us go down." " God smelled a sweet savor;" " God repented him that he had made man;" "and God said;" and

" walked ; " and " talked ; " and " rested." All these expressions are inconsistent with any other idea than that the person using them regarded God as having the form of man.

As a matter of fact, it is impossible for a man to conceive of a personal God, other than as a being having the human form. No one can think of an infinite being having the form of a horse, or of a bird, or of any animal beneath man. It is one of the necessities of the mind to associate forms with intellectual capacities. The highest form of which we have any conception is man's, and consequently, his is the only form that we can find in imagination to give to a personal God, because all other forms are, in our minds, connected with lower intelligences.

It is impossible to think of a personal God as a spirit without form. We can use these words, but they do not convey to the mind any real and tangible meaning. Every one who thinks of a personal God at all, thinks of him as having the human form. Take from God the idea of form ; speak of him simply as an all pervading spirit— which means an all pervading something about which we know nothing—and **Pantheism is the** result.

We are told that God made man; and the question naturally arises, how was this done? Was it by a process of "evolution," "development;" the "transmission of acquired habits;" the "survival of the fittest," or was the necessary amount of clay kneaded to the proper consistency, and then by the hands of God moulded into form? Modern science tells that man has been evolved, through countless epochs, from the lower forms; that he is the result of almost an infinite number of actions, reactions, experiences, states, forms, wants and adaptations. Did Moses intend to convey such a meaning, or did he believe that God took a sufficient amount of dust, made it the proper shape, and breathed into it the breath of life? Can any believer in the Bible give any reasonable account of this process of creation? Is it possible to imagine what was really done? Is there any theologian who will contend that man was created directly from the earth? Will he say that man was made substantially as he now is, with all his muscles properly developed for walking and speaking, and performing every variety of human action? That all his bones were formed as they now are, and all the relations of nerve, ligament, brain and motion as they are to-day?

Looking back over the history of animal life from the lowest to the highest forms, we find that there has been a slow and gradual development; a certain but constant relation between want and production; between use and form.   The Moner is said to be the simplest form of animal life that has yet been found. It has been described as "an organism without organs."   It is a kind of structureless structure ; a little mass of transparent jelly that can flatten itself out, and can expand and contract around its food. It can feed without a mouth, digest without a stomach, walk without feet, and reproduce itself by simple division.   By taking this Moner as the commencement of animal life, or rather as the first animal, it is easy to follow the development of the organic structure through all the forms of life to man himself. In this way finally every muscle, bone and joint, every organ, form and function may be accounted for. In this way, and in this way only, can the existence of rudimentary organs be explained.   Blot from the human mind the ideas of evolution, heredity, adaptation, and "the survival of the fittest," with which it has been enriched by Lamarck, Goethe, Darwin, Haeckel and Spencer, and all the facts in the history of animal life become utterly disconnected and meaningless.

Shall we throw away all that has been discovered with regard to organic life, and in its place take the statements of one who lived in the rude morning of a barbaric day? Will anybody now contend that man was a direct and independent creation, and sustains and bears no relation to the animals below him? Belief upon this subject must be governed at last by evidence. Man cannot believe as he pleases. He can control his speech, and can say that he believes or disbelieves; but after all, his will cannot depress or raise the scales with which his reason finds the worth and weight of facts. If this is not so, investigation, evidence, judgment and reason are but empty words.

I ask again, how were Adam and Eve created? In one account they are created male and female, and apparently at the same time. In the next account, Adam is made first, and Eve a long time afterwards, and from a part of the man. Did God simply by his creative fiat cause a rib slowly to expand, grow and divide into nerve, ligament, cartilage and flesh? How was the woman created from a rib? How was man created simply from dust? For my part, I cannot believe this statement. I may suffer for this in the world to come ; and may,

millions of years hence, sincerely wish that I had
never investigated the subject, but had been content
to take the ideas of the dead.   I do not believe that
any deity works in that way.   So far as my experience
goes, there is an unbroken procession of cause and
effect.   Each thing is a necessary link in an infinite
chain ; and I cannot conceive of this chain being
broken even for one instant.   Back of the simplest
moner there is a cause, and back of that another, and
so on, it seems to me, forever.   In my philosophy I
postulate neither beginning nor ending.

If the Mosaic account is true, we know how long
man has been upon this earth.   If that account can
be relied on, the first man was made about five
thousand eight hundred and eighty-three years ago.
Sixteen hundred and fifty-six years after the making
of the first man, the inhabitants of the world, with
the exception of eight people, were destroyed by a
flood.   This flood occurred only about four thousand
two hundred and twenty-seven years ago.   If this account is correct, at that time, only one kind of men
existed.   Noah and his family were certainly of the
same blood.   It therefore follows that all the differences
we see between the various races of men have been
caused in about four thousand years.   If the

account of the deluge is true, then since that event all the ancient kingdoms of the earth were founded, and their inhabitants passed through all the stages of savage, nomadic, barbaric and semi-civilized life ; through the epochs of Stone, Bronze and Iron ; established commerce, cultivated the arts, built cities, filled them with palaces and temples, invented writing, produced a literature and slowly fell to shapeless ruin. We must believe that all this has happened within a period of four thousand years.

From representations found upon Egyptian granite made more than three thousand years ago, we know that the negro was as black, his lips as full, and his hair as closely curled then as now. If we know anything, we know that there was at that time substantially the same difference between the Egyptian and the Negro as now. If we know anything, we know that magnificent statues were made in Egypt four thousand years before our era—that is to say, about six thousand years ago. There was at the World's Exposition, in the Egyptian department, a statue of king Cephren, known to have been chiseled more than six thousand years ago. In other words, if the Mosaic account must be believed, this statue was made before the world. We also know, if we know anything, that men lived in Europe with the hairy mammoth, the cave bear, the rhinoceros, and the hyena. Among the bones of these animals have been found the stone hatchets and flint arrows of our ancestors. In the caves where they lived have been discovered the remains of these animals that had been conquered, killed and devoured as food, hundreds of thousands of years ago.

If these facts are true, Moses was mistaken. For my part, I have infinitely more confidence in the discoveries of to-day, than in the records of a barbarous people. It will not now do to say that man has existed upon this earth for only about six thousand years. One can hardly compute in his imagination the time necessary for man to emerge from the barbarous state, naked and helpless, surrounded by animals far more powerful than he, to progress and finally create the civilizations of India, Egypt and Athens. The distance from savagery to Shakespeare must be measured not by hundreds, but by millions of years.

XIV.

SUNDAY.

" AND on the seventh day God ended his work which he had made, and he rested on the seventh day from all his work which he had made. And God blessed the seventh day and sanctified it; because that in it he had rested from all his work which God created and made."

The great work had been accomplished, the world, the sun, and moon, and all the hosts of heaven were finished; the earth was clothed in green, the seas were filled with life, the cattle wandered by the brooks—insects with painted wings were in the happy air, Adam and Eve were making each other's acquaintance, and God was resting from his work. He was contemplating the accomplishments of a week.

Because he rested on that day he sanctified it, and for that reason and for that alone, it was by the Jews considered a holy day. If he only rested on that day, there ought to be some account of what he did the following Monday.   Did he rest on that day? What did he do after he got rested?   Has he done anything in the way of creation since Saturday evening of the first week?

It is now claimed by the " scientific" Christians that the " days " of creation were not ordinary days of twenty-four hours each, but immensely long periods of time.   If they are right, then how long was the seventh day?   Was that, too, a geologic period covering thousands of ages?   That cannot be, because Adam and Eve were created the Saturday evening before, and according to the Bible that was about five thousand eight hundred and eighty-three years ago.   I cannot state the time exactly, because there have been as many as one hundred and forty different opinions given by learned Biblical students as to the time between the creation of the world and the birth of Christ.   We are quite certain, however, that, according to the Bible, it is not more than six thousand years since the creation of Adam.   From this it would appear that the seventh day was not a geologic epoch, but was in fact a period of less than six thousand years, and probably of only twenty-four hours.

The theologians who "answer" these things may take their choice. If they take the ground that the "days" were periods of twenty-four hours, then geology will force them to throw away the whole account. If, on the other hand, they admit that the days were vast "periods," then the sacredness of the Sabbath must be given up.

There is found in the Bible no intimation that there was the least difference in the days. They are all spoken of in the same way. It may be replied that our translation is incorrect. If this is so, then only those who understand Hebrew, have had a revelation from God, and all the rest have been deceived.

How is it possible to sanctify a space of time? Is rest holier than labor? If there is any difference between days, ought not that to be considered best in which the most useful labor has been performed?

Of all the superstitions of mankind, this insanity about the "sacred Sabbath" is the most absurd. The idea of feeling it a duty to be solemn and sad one-seventh of the time! To think that we can please an infinite being by staying in some dark and sombre room, instead of walking in the perfumed fields! Why should God hate to see a man happy? Why

should it excite his wrath to see a family in the
woods, by some babbling stream, talking, laughing
and loving?   Nature works on that "sacred" day.
The earth turns, the rivers run, the trees grow, buds
burst into flower, and birds fill the air with song.
Why should we look sad, and think about death, and
hear about hell?   Why should that day be filled with
gloom instead of joy?

A poor mechanic, working all the week in dust
and noise, needs a day of rest and joy, a day to visit
stream and wood—a day to live with wife and child ;
a day in which to laugh at care, and gather hope and
strength for toils to come.   And his weary wife needs
a breath of sunny air, away from street and wall,
amid the hills or by the margin of the sea, where she
can sit and prattle with her babe, and fill with happy
dreams the long, glad day.

The " Sabbath " was born of asceticism, hatred
of human joy, fanaticism, ignorance, egotism of
priests and the cowardice of the people.   This day,
for thousands of years, has been dedicated to superstition, to the dissemination of mistakes, and the
establishment of falsehoods.   Every Freethinker,
as a matter of duty, should violate this day.   He
should assert his independence, and do all within his

power to wrest the Sabbath from the gloomy church and give it back to liberty and joy. Freethinkers should make the Sabbath a day of mirth and music ; a day to spend with wife and child—a day of games, and books, and dreams—a day to put fresh flowers above our sleeping dead—a day of memory and hope, of love and rest.

Why should we in this age of the world be dominated by the dead? Why should barbarian Jews who went down to death and dust three thousand years ago, control the living world? Why should we care for the superstition of men who began the Sabbath by paring their nails, "beginning at the fourth finger, then going to the second, then to the fifth, then to the third, and ending with the thumb?" How pleasing to God this must have been. The Jews were very careful of these nail parings. They who threw them upon the ground were wicked, because Satan used them to work evil upon the earth. They believed that upon the Sabbath, souls were allowed to leave purgatory and cool their burning souls in water. Fires were neither allowed to be kindled nor extinguished, and upon that day it was a sin to bind up wounds. " The lame might use a staff, but the blind could not." So strict was the

Sabbath kept, that at one time " if a Jew on a journey
was overtaken by the ' sacred day ' in a wood, or on
the highway, no matter where, nor under what
circumstances, he must sit down," and there remain
until the day was gone. " If he fell down in the
dirt, there he was compelled to stay until the day
was done."   For violating the Sabbath, the punishment was death, for nothing short of the offender's
blood could satisfy the wrath of God.   There are, in
the Old Testament, two reasons given for abstaining
from labor on the Sabbath :—the resting of God, and
the redemption of the Jews from the bondage of
Egypt.

Since the establishment of the Christian religion,
the day has been changed, and Christians do not
regard the day as holy upon which God actually
rested, and which he sanctified.   The Christian
Sabbath, or the " Lord's day " was legally established
by the murderer Constantine, because upon that day
Christ was supposed to have risen from the dead.

It is not easy to see where Christians got the
right to disregard the direct command of God, to
labor on the day he sanctified, and keep as sacred, a
day upon which he commanded men to labor.   The
Sabbath of God is Saturday, and if any day is to be

kept holy, that is the one, and not the Sunday of the Christian.

Let us throw away these superstitions and take the higher, nobler ground, that every day should be rendered sacred by some loving act, by increasing the happinesss of man, giving birth to noble thoughts, putting in the path of toil some flower of joy, helping the unfortunate, lifting the fallen, dispelling gloom, destroying prejudice, defending the helpless and filling homes with light and love.

XV.

THE NECESSITY FOR A GOOD MEMORY.

IT must not be forgotten that there are two accounts of the creation in Genesis. The first account stops with the third verse of the second chapter. The chapters have been improperly divided. In the original Hebrew the Pentateuch was neither divided into chapters nor verses. There was not even any system of punctuation. It was written wholly with consonants, without vowels, and without any marks, dots, or lines to indicate them.

These accounts are materially different, and both cannot be true. Let us see wherein they differ.

The second account of the creation begins with the fourth verse of the second chapter, and is as follows :

"These are the generations of the heavens and of the earth when they were created, in the day that the Lord God made the earth and the heavens.

" And every plant of the field before it was in the earth, and every herb of the field before it grew ; for the Lord God had not caused it to rain upon the earth, and there was not a man to till the ground.

" But there went up a mist from the earth and watered the whole face of the ground.

" And the Lord God formed man of the dust of the ground, and breathed into his nostrils the breath of life ; and man became a living soul.

" And the Lord God planted a garden eastward in Eden ; and there he put the man whom he had formed.

" And out of the ground made the Lord God to grow every tree that is pleasant to the sight, and good for food ; the tree of life also in the midst of the garden, and the tree of knowledge of good and evil.

" And a river went out of Eden to water the garden ; and from thence it was parted and became into four heads.

" The name of the first is Pison ; that is it which compasseth the whole land of Havilah, where there is gold.

" And the gold of that land is good : there is bdellium and the onyx stone.

" And the name of the second river is Gihon :
the same is it that compasseth the whole land of
Ethiopia.

" And the name of the third river is Hiddekel ;
that is it which goeth toward the east of Assyria.
And the fourth river is Euphrates.

"And the Lord God took the man, and put him
into the Garden of Eden to dress it and to keep it.

" And the Lord God commanded the man,
saying, Of every tree of the garden thou mayest freely
eat; But of the tree of the knowledge of good and
evil, thou shalt not eat of it ; for in the day that
thou eatest thereof thou shalt surely die.

" And the Lord God said, It is not good that the
man should be alone ; I will make him an helpmeet
for him.

" And out of the ground the Lord God formed
every beast of the field, and every fowl of the air ;
and brought them unto Adam to see what he would
call them : and whatsoever Adam called every living
creature, that was the name thereof.

" And Adam gave names to all cattle, and to the
fowl of the air, and to every beast of the field ; but
for Adam there was not found a helpmeet for
him.

" And the Lord God caused a deep sleep to fall upon Adam, and he slept ; and he took one of his ribs, and closed up the flesh instead thereof ;

" And the rib, which the Lord God had taken from man, made he a woman and brought her unto the man.

"And Adam said, This is now bone of my bones, and flesh of my flesh ; she shall be called Woman, because she was taken out of man.

"Therefore shall a man leave his father and his mother, and shall cleave unto his wife ; and they shall be one flesh.

" And they were both naked, the man and his wife, and were not ashamed."

ORDER OF CREATION IN THE FIRST ACCOUNT :

1. The heaven and the earth, and light were made.

2. The firmament was constructed and the waters divided.

3. The waters gathered into seas—and then came dry land, grass, herbs and fruit trees.

4. The sun and moon.   He made the stars also.

5. Fishes, fowls, and great whales.

6. Beasts, cattle, every creeping thing, man and woman.

ORDER OF CREATION IN THE SECOND ACCOUNT :

1.   The heavens and the earth.

2.   A mist went up from the earth, and watered the whole face of the ground.

3.   Created a man out of dust, by the name of Adam.

4.   Planted a garden eastward in Eden, and put the man in it.

5.   Created the beasts and fowls.

6.   Created a woman out of one of the man's ribs.

In the second account, man was made *before* the beasts and fowls.   If this is true, the first account is false.   And if the theologians of our time are correct in their view that the Mosaic day means thousands of ages, then, according to the second account, Adam existed millions of years before Eve was formed. He must have lived one Mosaic day before there were any trees, and another Mosaic day before the beasts and fowls were created.   Will some kind clergymen tell us upon what kind of food Adam subsisted during these immense periods?

In the second account a man is made, and the fact that he was without a helpmeet did not occur to

the Lord God until a couple "of vast periods" afterwards. The Lord God suddenly coming to an
appreciation of the situation said, "It is not good that
the man should be alone. I will make him an helpmeet for him."

Now, after concluding to make "an helpmeet" for
Adam, what did the Lord God do? Did he at once
proceed to make a woman? No. What did he do?
He made the beasts, and tried to induce Adam to
take one of them for "an helpmeet." If I am
incorrect, read the following account, and tell me
what it means :

"And the Lord God said, It is not good that the
man should be alone; I will make him an helpmeet
for him.

"And out of the ground the Lord God
formed every beast of the field, and every fowl
of the air; and brought them unto Adam to see
what he would call them : and whatsoever Adam
called every living creature, that was the name
thereof.

"And Adam gave names to all cattle, and to
the fowl of the air, and to every beast of the field ;
but for Adam there was not found an helpmeet
for him."

Unless the Lord God was looking for an helpmeet for Adam, why did he cause the animals to
pass before him? And why did he, after the
menagerie had passed by, pathetically exclaim,
" But for Adam there was not found an helpmeet
for him "?

It seems that Adam saw nothing that struck his
fancy. The fairest ape, the sprightliest chimpanzee,
the loveliest baboon, the most bewitching orang-
outang, the most fascinating gorilla failed to touch
with love's sweet pain, poor Adam's lonely heart.
Let us rejoice that this was so. Had he fallen in
love then, there never would have been a Freethinker in this world.

Dr. Adam Clarke, speaking of this remarkable
proceeding says :—"God caused the animals to pass
before Adam to show him that no creature yet formed
could make him a suitable companion; that Adam
was convinced that none of these animals could be
a suitable companion for him, and that therefore
he must continue in a state that was not good
(celibacy) unless he became a further debtor to
the bounty of his maker, for among all the animals
which he had formed, there was not a helpmeet
for Adam."

Upon this same subject, Dr. Scott informs us "that it was not conducive to the happiness of the man to remain without the consoling society, and endearment of tender friendship, nor consistent with the end of his creation to be without marriage by which the earth might be replenished and worshipers and servants raised up to render him praise and glory. Adam seems to have been vastly better acquainted by intuition or revelation with the distinct properties of every creature than the most sagacious observer since the fall of man.

"Upon this review of the animals, not one was found in outward form his counterpart, nor one suited to engage his affections, participate in his enjoyments, or associate with him in the worship of God."

Dr. Matthew Henry admits that "God brought all the animals together to see if there was a suitable match for Adam in any of the numerous families of the inferior creatures, but there was none. They were all looked over, but Adam could not be matched among them all. Therefore God created a new thing to be a helpmeet for him."

Failing to satisfy Adam with any of the inferior animals, the Lord God caused a deep sleep to fall upon him, and while in this sleep took out one of

Adam's ribs and "closed up the flesh instead thereof."
And out of this rib, the Lord God made a woman,
and brought her to the man.

Was the Lord God compelled to take a part of
the man because he had used up all the original
"nothing" out of which the universe was made? Is
it possible for any sane and intelligent man to believe
this story? Must a man be born a second time
before this account seems reasonable?

Imagine the Lord God with a bone in his hand
with which to start a woman, trying to make up his
mind whether to make a blonde or a brunette!

Just at this point it may be proper for me to
warn all persons from laughing at or making light of,
any stories found in the " Holy Bible." When you
come to die, every laugh will be a thorn in your
pillow. At that solemn moment, as you look back
upon the records of your life, no matter how many
men you may have wrecked and ruined ; no matter
how many women you have deceived and deserted,
all that can be forgiven ; but if you remember then
that you have laughed at even one story in God's
" sacred book " you will see through the gathering
shadows of death the forked tongues of devils, and
the leering eyes of fiends.

These stories must be believed, or the work of regeneration can never be commenced. No matter how well you act your part, live as honestly as you may, clothe the naked, feed the hungry, divide your last farthing with the poor, and you are simply traveling the broad road that leads inevitably to eternal death, unless at the same time you implicitly believe the Bible to be the inspired word of God.

Let me show you the result of unbelief. Let us suppose, for a moment, that we are at the Day of Judgment, listening to the trial of souls as they arrive. The Recording Secretary, or whoever does the cross-examining, says to a soul:

Where are you from?

I am from the Earth.

What kind of a man were you?

Well, I don't like to talk about myself. I suppose you can tell by looking at your books.

No, sir. You must tell what kind of a man you were.

Well, I was what you might call a first-rate fellow. I loved my wife and children. My home was my heaven. My fireside was a paradise to me. To sit there and see the lights and shadows fall upon the faces of those I loved, was to me a perfect joy.

How did you treat your family?

I never said an unkind word. I never caused my wife, nor one of my children, a moment's pain.

Did you pay your debts?

I did not owe a dollar when I died, and left enough to pay my funeral expenses, and to keep the fierce wolf of want from the door of those I loved.

Did you belong to any church?

No, sir. They were too narrow, pinched and bigoted for me, I never thought that I could be very happy if other folks were damned.

Did you believe in eternal punishment?

Well, no. I always thought that God could get his revenge in far less time.

Did you believe the rib story?

Do you mean the Adam and Eve business?

Yes! Did you believe that?

To tell you the God's truth, that was just a little more than I could swallow.

Away with him to hell!

Next!

Where are you from?

I am from the world too.

Did you belong to any church?

Yes, sir, and to the Young Men's Christian Association besides.

What was your business?

Cashier in a Savings Bank.

Did you ever run away with any money?

Where I came from, a witness could not be compelled to criminate himself.

The law is different here. Answer the question. Did you run away with any money?

Yes, sir.

How much?

One hundred thousand dollars.

Did you take anything else with you?

Yes, sir.

Well, what else?

I took my neighbor's wife—we sang together in the choir.

Did you have a wife and children of your own?

Yes, sir.

And you deserted them?

Yes, sir, but such was my confidence in God that I believed he would take care of them.

Have you heard of them since?

No, sir.

Did you believe in the rib story?

Bless your soul, of course I did.   A thousand times I regretted that there were no harder stories in the Bible, so that I could have shown my wealth of faith.

Do you believe the rib story yet?

Yes, with all my heart.

Give him a harp!

Well, as I was saying, God made a woman from Adam's rib.   Of course, I do not know exactly how this was done, but when he got the woman finished, he presented her to Adam.   He liked her, and they commenced house-keeping in the celebrated Garden of Eden.

Must we, in order to be good, gentle and loving in our lives, believe that the creation of woman was a second thought?   That Jehovah really endeavored to induce Adam to take one of the lower animals as an helpmeet for him?   After all, is it not possible to live honest and courageous lives without believing these fables?   It is said that from Mount Sinai God gave, amid thunderings and lightnings, ten command- ments for the guidance of mankind ; and yet among them is not found—" Thou shalt believe the Bible."

XVI.

THE GARDEN.

I N the first account we are told that God made
man, male and female, and said to them " Be
fruitful, and multiply, and replenish the earth and
subdue it."

In the second account only the man is made, and
he is put in a garden "to dress it and to keep it."
He is not told to subdue the earth, but to dress and
keep a garden.

In the first account man is given every herb
bearing seed upon the face of the earth and the fruit
of every tree for food, and in the second, he is given
only the fruit of all the trees in the garden with the
exception "of the tree of the knowledge of good and
evil" which was a deadly poison.

There was issuing from this garden a river that
was parted into four heads. The first of these, Pison,
compassed the whole land of Havilah, the second,
Gihon, that compassed the whole land of Ethiopia,

the third, Heddekel, that flowed toward the east of
Assyria, and the fourth, the Euphrates. Where are
these four rivers now? The brave prow of discovery
has visited every sea; the traveler has pressed with
weary feet the soil of every clime; and yet there has
been found no place from which four rivers sprang.
The Euphrates still journeys to the gulf, but where
are Pison, Gihon and the mighty Heddekel? Surely
by going to the source of the Euphrates we ought to
find either these three rivers or their ancient beds.
Will some minister when he answers the " Mistakes
of Moses" tell us where these rivers are or were?
The maps of the world are incomplete without these
mighty streams. We have discovered the sources
of the Nile ; the North Pole will soon be touched by
an American ; but these three rivers still rise in
unknown hills, still flow through unknown lands, and
empty still in unknown seas.

The account of these four rivers is what the
Rev. David Swing would call "a geographical
poem." The orthodox clergy cover the whole
affair with the blanket of allegory, while the
"scientific" Christian folks talk about cataclysms,
upheavals, earthquakes, and vast displacements of
the earth's crust.

The question, then arises, whether within the last six thousand years there have been such upheavals and displacements? Talk as you will about the vast "creative periods" that preceded the appearance of man; it is, according to the Bible, only about six thousand years since man was created. Moses gives us the generations of men from Adam until his day, and this account cannot be explained away by calling centuries, days.

According to the second account of creation, these four rivers were made after the creation of man, and consequently they must have been obliterated by convulsions of Nature within six thousand years.

Can we not account for these contradictions, absurdities, and falsehoods by simply saying that although the writer may have done his level best, he failed because he was limited in knowledge, led away by tradition, and depended too implicitly upon the correctness of his imagination? Is not such a course far more reasonable than to insist that all these things are true and must stand though every science shall fall to mental dust?

Can any reason be given for not allowing man to eat of the fruit of the tree of knowledge? What kind of tree was that? If it is all an allegory, what truth is sought to be conveyed? Why should God object to that fruit being eaten by man? Why did he put it in the midst of the garden? There was certainly plenty of room outside. If he wished to keep man and this tree apart, why did he put them together? And why, after he had eaten, was he thrust out? The only answer that we have a right to give, is the one given in the Bible. " And the Lord God said, Behold the man has become as one of us to know good and evil; and now, lest he put forth his hand and take also of the tree of life, and eat, and live forever: Therefore the Lord God sent him forth from the Garden of Eden, to till the ground from whence he was taken."

Will some minister, some graduate of Andover, tell us what this means? Are we bound to believe it without knowing what the meaning is? If it is a revelation, what does it reveal? Did God object to education then, and does that account for the hostile attitude still assumed by theologians toward all scientific truth? Was there in the garden a tree of life, the eating of which would have rendered Adam and Eve immortal? Is it true, that after the Lord God drove them from the garden that he placed upon its Eastern side " Cherubim and a flaming

sword which turned every way to keep the way of
the tree of life?" Are the Cherubim and the
flaming sword guarding that tree still, or was it
destroyed, or did its rotting trunk, as the Rev.
Robert Collyer suggests, "nourish a bank of
violets"?

What objection could God have had to the
immortality of man? You see that after all, this
sacred record, instead of assuring us of immortality,
shows us only how we lost it. In this there is
assuredly but little consolation.

According to this story we have lost one Eden,
but nowhere in the Mosaic books are we told how
we may gain another. I know that the Christians
tell us there is another, in which all true believers
will finally be gathered, and enjoy the unspeakable
happiness of seeing the unbelievers in hell ; but they
do not tell us where it is.

Some commentators say that the Garden of
Eden was in the third heaven—some in the fourth,
others have located it in the moon, some in the air
beyond the attraction of the earth, some on the
earth, some under the earth, some inside the earth,
some at the North Pole, others at the South, some
in Tartary, some in China, some on the borders of

the Ganges, some in the island of Ceylon, some in
Armenia, some in Africa, some under the Equator,
others in Mesopotamia, in Syria, Persia, Arabia,
Babylon, Assyria, Palestine and Europe.   Others
have contended that it was invisible, that it was an
allegory, and must be spiritually understood.

But whether you understand these things or not,
you must believe them.   You may be laughed at in
this world for insisting that God put Adam into a
deep sleep and made a woman out of one of his ribs,
but you will be crowned and glorified in the next.
You will also have the pleasure of hearing the
gentlemen howl there, who laughed at you here.
While you will not be permitted to take any revenge,
you will be allowed to smilingly express your entire
acquiescence in the will of God.   But where is the
new Eden?   No one knows.   The one was lost, and
the other has not been found.

Is it true that man was once perfectly pure and
innocent, and that he became degenerate by disobe-
dience?   No.   The real truth is, and the history of
man shows, that he has advanced.   Events, like the
pendulum of a clock have swung forward and back
ward, but after all, man, like the hands, has gone
steadily on.   Man is growing grander.   He is not

degenerating. Nations and individuals fail and die, and make room for higher forms. The intellectual horizon of the world widens as the centuries pass. Ideals grow grander and purer; the difference between justice and mercy becomes less and less; liberty enlarges, and love intensifies as the years sweep on. The ages of force and fear, of cruelty and wrong, are behind us and the real Eden is beyond. It is said that a desire for knowledge lost us the Eden of the past; but whether that is true or not, it will certainly give us the Eden of the future.

XVII.

THE FALL.

WE are told that the serpent was more subtle than any beast of the field, that he had a conversation with Eve, in which he gave his opinion about the effect of eating certain fruit; that he assured her it was good to eat, that it was pleasant to the eye, that it would make her wise; that she was induced to take some; that she persuaded her husband to try it; that God found it out, that he then cursed the snake; condemning it to crawl and eat the dust; that he multiplied the sorrows of Eve, cursed the ground for Adam's sake, started thistles and thorns, condemned man to eat the herb of the field in the sweat of his face, pronounced the curse of death, "Dust thou art and unto dust shalt thou return," made coats of skins for Adam and Eve, and drove them out of Eden.

Who, and what was this serpent? Dr. Adam Clarke says :—" The serpent must have walked erect.

for this is necessarily implied in his punishment. That he was endued with the gift of speech, also with reason. That these things were given to this creature. The woman no doubt having often seen him walking erect, and talking and reasoning, therefore she testifies no sort of surprise when he accosts her in the language related in the text. It therefore appears to me that a creature of the ape or orang-outang kind is here intended, and that Satan made use of this creature as the most proper instrument for the accomplishment of his murderous purposes against the life of the soul of man. Under this creature he lay hid, and by this creature he seduced our first parents. Such a creature answers to every part of the description in the text. It is evident from the structure of its limbs and its muscles that it might have been originally designed to walk erect, and that nothing else than the sovereign controlling power could induce it to put down hands—in every respect formed like those of man—and walk like those creatures whose claw-armed parts prove them to have been designed to walk on all fours. The stealthy cunning, and endless variety of the pranks and tricks of these creatures show them even now to be wiser and more intelligent than any other creature,

man alone excepted.   Being obliged to walk on all
fours and gather their food from the ground, they are
literally obliged to eat the dust ; and though
exceeding cunning, and careful in a variety of
instances to separate that part which is wholesome
and proper for food from that which is not so, in the
article of cleanliness they are lost to all sense of
propriety.   Add to this their utter aversion to walk
upright; it requires the utmost discipline to bring
them to it, and scarcely anything offends or irritates
them more than to be obliged to do it.   Long
observation of these animals enables me to state
these facts.   For earnest, attentive watching, and for
chattering and babbling they (the ape) have no
fellows in the animal world.   Indeed, the ability and
propensity to chatter, is all they have left of their
original gift of speech, of which they appear to have
been deprived at the fall as a part of their punishment."

Here then is the " connecting link " between
man and the lower creation. The serpent was
simply an orang-outang that spoke Hebrew with the
greatest ease, and had the outward appearance of a
perfect gentleman, seductive in manner, plausible,
polite, and most admirably calculated to deceive.

It never did seem reasonable to me that a long, cold and disgusting snake with an apple in his mouth, could deceive anybody ; and I am glad, even at this late date to know that the something that persuaded Eve to taste the forbidden fruit was, at least, in the shape of a man.

Dr. Henry does not agree with the zoological explanation of Mr. Clark, but insists that "it is certain that the devil that beguiled Eve is the old serpent, a malignant by creation, an angel of light, an immediate attendant upon God's throne, but by sin an apostate from his first state, and a rebel against God's crown and dignity. He who attacked our first parents was surely the prince of devils, the ring leader in rebellion. The devil chose to act his part in a serpent, because it is a specious creature, has a spotted, dappled skin, and then, went erect. Perhaps it was a flying serpent which seemed to come from on high, as a messenger from the upper world, one of the seraphim ; because the serpent is a subtile creature. What Eve thought of this serpent speaking to her, we are not likely to tell, and, I believe, she herself did not know what to think of it. At first, perhaps, she supposed it might be a good angel, and yet afterwards might suspect something

amiss. The person tempted was a woman, now
alone, and at a distance from her husband, but near
the forbidden tree. It was the devil's subtlety to
assault the weaker vessel with his temptations, as we
may suppose her inferior to Adam in knowledge,
strength and presence of mind. Some think that
Eve received the command not immediately from
God, but at second hand from her husband, and
might, therefore, be the more easily persuaded to
discredit it. It was the policy of the devil to enter
into discussion with her when she was alone. He
took advantage by finding her near the forbidden
tree. God permitted Satan to prevail over Eve,
for wise and holy ends. Satan teaches men first to
doubt, and then to deny. He makes skeptics first,
and by degrees makes them atheists."

We are compelled to admit that nothing could
be more attractive to a woman than a snake walking
erect, with a " spotted, dappled skin," unless it were
a serpent with wings. Is it not humiliating to know
that our ancestors believed these things? Why
should we object to the Darwinian doctrine of descent
after this?

Our fathers thought it their duty to believe,
thought it a sin to entertain the slightest doubt, and

really supposed that their credulity was exceedingly
gratifying to God.   To them, the story was entirely
real.   They could see the garden, hear the babble of
waters, smell the perfume of flowers.   They believed
there was a tree where knowledge grew like plums
or pears ; and they could plainly see the serpent
coiled amid its rustling leaves, coaxing Eve to violate
the laws of God.

Where did the serpent come from ?   On which
of the six days was he created ?   Who made him ?
Is it possible that God would make a successful rival ?
He must have known that Adam and Eve would fall.
He knew what a snake with a "spotted, dappled skin "
could do with an inexperienced woman.   Why did
he not defend his children ?   He knew that if the
serpent got into the garden, Adam and Eve would
sin, that he would have to drive them out, that afterwards the world would be destroyed, and that he
himself would die upon the cross.

Again, I ask what and who was this serpent ?
He was not a man, for only one man had been made.
He was not a woman.   He was not a beast of the
field, because " he was more subtile than any beast
of the field which the Lord God had made."   He
was neither fish nor fowl, nor snake, because he had

the power of speech, and did not crawl upon his
belly until after he was cursed. Where did this
serpent come from? Why was he not kept out of
the garden? Why did not the Lord God take him
by the tail and snap his head off? Why did he not
put Adam and Eve on their guard about this serpent?
They, of course, were not acquainted in the neighbor-
hood, and knew nothing about the serpent's reputation
for truth and veracity among his neighbors. Probably Adam saw him when he was looking for " an
helpmeet" and gave him a name, but Eve had never
met him before. She was not surprised to hear a
serpent talk, as that was the first one she had ever
met. Every thing being new to her, and her husband
not being with her just at that moment, it need hardly
excite our wonder that she tasted the fruit by way of
experiment. Neither should we be surprised that
when she saw it was good and pleasant to the eye,
and a fruit to be desired to make one wise, she had
the generosity to divide with her husband.

Theologians have filled thousands of volumes
with abuse of this serpent, but it seems that he told
the exact truth. We are told that this serpent was,
in fact, Satan, the greatest enemy of mankind, and
that he entered the serpent, appearing to our first

parents in its body. If this is so, why should the
serpent have been cursed? Why should God curse
the serpent for what had really been done by the
devil? Did Satan remain in the body of the serpent,
and in some mysterious manner share his punishment? Is it true that when we kill a snake we also
destroy an evil spirit, or is there but one devil, and
did he perish at the death of the first serpent? Is it
on account of that transaction in the Garden of Eden,
that all the descendants of Adam and Eve known as
Jews and Christians hate serpents?

Do you account for the snake-worship in Mexico,
Africa and India in the same way?

What was the form of the serpent when he
entered the garden, and in what way did he move
from place to place? Did he walk or fly? Certainly
he did not crawl, because that mode of locomotion
was pronounced upon him as a curse. Upon what
food did he subsist before his conversation with Eve?
We know that after that he lived upon dust, but
what did he eat before? It may be that this is all
poetic; and the truest poetry is, according to Touch-
stone, " the most feigning."

In this same chapter we are informed that " unto
Adam also and to his wife did the Lord God make

coats of skins and clothed them." Where did the Lord God get those skins? He must have taken them from the animals; he was a butcher. Then he had to prepare them; he was a tanner. Then he made them into coats; he was a tailor. How did it happen that they needed coats of skins, when they had been perfectly comfortable in a nude condition? Did the "fall" produce a change in the climate?

Is it really necessary to believe this account in order to be happy here, or hereafter? Does it tend to the elevation of the human race to speak of "God" as a butcher, tanner and tailor?

And here, let me say once for all, that when I speak of God, I mean the being described by Moses; the Jehovah of the Jews. There may be for aught I know, somewhere in the unknown shoreless vast, some being whose dreams are constellations and within whose thought the infinite exists. About this being, if such an one exists, I have nothing to say. He has written no books, inspired no barbarians, required no worship, and has prepared no hell in which to burn the honest seeker after truth.

When I speak of God, I mean that god who prevented man from putting forth his hand and taking also of the fruit of the tree of life that he might live forever; of that god who multiplied the agonies of woman, increased the weary toil of man, and in his anger drowned a world—of that god whose altars reeked with human blood, who butchered babes, violated maidens, enslaved men and filled the earth with cruelty and crime; of that god who made heaven for the few, hell for the many, and who wi'll gloat forever and ever upon the writhings of the lost and damned.

XVIII.

DAMPNESS.

"And it came to pass, when men began to multiply on the face of the earth, and daughters were born unto them.

"That the sons of God saw the daughters of men that they were fair; and they took them wives of all which they chose.

"And the Lord said, My spirit shall not always strive with man, for that he also is flesh; yet his days shall be an hundred and twenty years.

"There were giants in the earth in those days; and also after that when the sons of God came in unto the daughters of men, and they bare children to them, the same became mighty men which were of old, men of renown.

"And God saw that the wickedness of man was great in the earth, and that every imagination of the thoughts of his heart was only evil continually.

"And it repented the Lord that he had made man on the earth, and it grieved him at his heart.

"And the Lord said, I will destroy man whom I have created from the face of the earth; both man, and beast, and the creeping thing, and the fowls of the air; for it repenteth me that I have made them."

From this account it seems that driving Adam and Eve out of Eden did not have the effect to improve them or their children. On the contrary, the world grew worse and worse. They were under the immediate control and government of God, and he from time to time made known his will; but in spite of this, man continued to increase in crime.

Nothing in particular seems to have been done. Not a school was established. There was no written language. There was not a Bible in the world. The "scheme of salvation" was kept a profound secret. The five points of Calvinism had not been taught. Sunday schools had not been opened. In short, nothing had been done for the reformation of the world. God did not even keep his own sons at home, but allowed them to leave their abode in the firmament, and make love to the daughters of men. As a result of this, the world was filled with wickedness and giants to such an extent that God regretted "that he had made man on the earth, and it grieved him at his heart."

Of course God knew when he made man, that he would afterwards regret it. He knew that the people would grow worse and worse until destruction would be the only remedy. He knew that he would have to kill all except Noah and his family, and it is hard to see why he did not make Noah and his family in the first place, and leave Adam and Eve in the original dust. He knew that they would be tempted, that he would have to drive them out of the garden to keep them from eating of the tree of life ; that the whole thing would be a failure ; that Satan would defeat his plan ; that he could not reform the people ; that his own sons would corrupt them, and that at last he would have to drown them all except Noah and his family. Why was the Garden of Eden planted ? Why was the experiment made ? Why were Adam and Eve exposed to the seductive arts of the serpent ? Why did God wait until the cool of the day before looking after his children ? Why was he not on hand in the morning ?

Why did he fill the world with his own children, knowing that he would have to destroy them? And why does this same God tell me how to raise my children when he had to drown his?

It is a little curious that when God wished to reform the ante-diluvian world he said nothing about hell; that he had no revivals, no camp-meetings, no tracts, no outpourings of the Holy Ghost, no baptisms, no noon prayer meetings, and never mentioned the great doctrine of salvation by faith. If the orthodox creeds of the world are true, all those people went to hell without ever having heard that such a place existed. If eternal torment is a fact, surely these miserable wretches ought to have been warned. They were threatened only with water when they were in fact doomed to eternal fire!

Is it not strange that God said nothing to Adam and Eve about a future life; that he should have kept these "infinite verities" to himself and allowed millions to live and die without the hope of heaven, or the fear of hell?

It may be that hell was not made at that time. In the six days of creation nothing is said about the construction of a bottomless pit, and the serpent himself did not make his appearance until after the

creation of man and woman.   Perhaps he was made
on the first Sunday, and from that fact came, it may
be, the old couplet,

> "And Satan still some mischief finds
> For idle hands to do."

The sacred historian failed also to tell us when
the cherubim and the flaming sword were made, and
said nothing about two of the persons composing the
Trinity.   It certainly would have been an easy thing
to enlighten Adam and his immediate descendants.
The world was then only about fifteen hundred and
thirty-six years old, and only about three or four
generations of men had lived.   Adam had been dead
only about six hundred and six years, and some of
his grandchildren must, at that time, have been alive
and well.

It is hard to see why God did not civilize these
people.   He certainly had the power to use, and the
wisdom to devise the proper means.   What right
has a god to fill a world with fiends?   Can there be
goodness in this?   Why should he make experiments that he knows must fail?   Is there wisdom in
this?   And what right has a man to charge an
infinite being with wickedness and folly?

According to Moses, God made up his mind not only to destroy the people, but the beasts and the creeping things, and the fowls of the air. What had the beasts, and the creeping things, and the birds done to excite the anger of God? Why did he repent having made them? Will some Christian give us an explanation of this matter? No good man will inflict unnecessary pain upon a beast; how then can we worship a god who cares nothing for the agonies of the dumb creatures that he made?

Why did he make animals that he knew he would destroy? Does God delight in causing pain? He had the power to make the beasts, and fowls, and creeping things in his own good time and way, and it is to be presumed that he made them according to his wish. Why should he destroy them? They had committed no sin. They had eaten no forbidden fruit, made no aprons, nor tried to reach the tree of life. Yet this god, in blind unreasoning wrath destroyed "all flesh wherein was the breath of life, and every living thing beneath the sky, and every substance wherein was life that he had made."

Jehovah having made up his mind to drown the world, told Noah to make an Ark of gopher wood three hundred cubits long, fifty cubits wide and thirty cubits high.   A cubit is twenty-two inches ; so that the ark was five hundred and fifty feet long, ninety-one feet and eight inches wide and fifty-five feet high.   This ark was divided into three stories, and had on top, one window twenty-two inches square. Ventilation   must   have   been   one   of   Jehovah's hobbies.   Think of a ship larger than the Great Eastern with only one window, and that but twenty-two inches square !

The ark also had one door set in the side thereof that shut from the outside.   As soon as this ship was finished, and properly victualed, Noah received seven days notice to get the animals in the ark.

It is claimed by some of the scientific theologians that the flood was partial, that the waters covered only a small portion of the world, and that consequently only a few animals were in the ark.   It is impossible to conceive of language that can more clearly convey the idea of a universal flood than that found in the inspired account.   If the flood was only partial, why did God say he would "destroy all flesh wherein is the breath of life from under heaven, and that every thing that is in the earth shall die"? Why did he say "I will destroy man whom I have created from the face of the earth, both man and beast, and the creeping thing and the fowls of the air"? Why did he say "And every living substance that I have made will I destroy from off the face of the earth"? Would a partial, local flood have fulfilled these threats?

Nothing can be clearer than that the writer of this account intended to convey, and did convey the idea that the flood was universal. Why should Christians try to deprive God of the glory of having wrought the most stupendous of miracles? Is it possible that the Infinite could not overwhelm with waves this atom called the earth? Do you doubt his power, his wisdom or his justice?

Believers in miracles should not endeavor to explain them. There is but one way to explain anything, and that is to account for it by natural agencies. The moment you explain a miracle, it disappears. You should depend not upon explanation, but assertion. You should not be driven from the field because the miracle is shown to be unreasonable. You should reply that all miracles are unreasonable. Neither should you be in the least disheartened if it is shown to be impossible. The possible is not miraculous. You should take the ground that if miracles were reasonable, and possible, there would be no reward paid for believing them. The Christian has the goodness to believe, while the sinner asks for evidence. It is enough for God to work miracles without being called upon to substantiate them for the benefit of unbelievers.

Only a few years ago, the Christians believed implicitly in the literal truth of every miracle recorded in the Bible. Whoever tried to explain them in some natural way, was looked upon as an infidel in disguise, but now he is regarded as a benefactor. The credulity of the church is decreasing, and the most marvelous miracles are now either "explained," or allowed to take refuge behind the mistakes of the translators, or hide in the drapery of allegory.

In the sixth chapter, Noah is ordered to take "of every living thing of all flesh, two of every sort into the ark—male and female." In the seventh chapter the order is changed, and Noah is commanded, according to the Protestant Bible, as follows: " Of every clean beast thou shalt take to thee by sevens, the male and his female, and of beasts that are not clean, by two, the male and his female. Of fowls also of the air by sevens, the male and the female."

According to the Catholic Bible, Noah was commanded—"Of all clean beasts take seven and seven, the male and the female. But of the beasts that are unclean two and two, the male and the female. Of the fowls also of the air seven and seven, the male and the female."

For the purpose of belittling this miracle, many commentators have taken the ground that Noah was not ordered to take seven males and seven females of each kind of clean beasts, but seven in all. Many Christians contend that only seven clean beasts of each kind were taken into the ark—three and a half of each sex.

If the account in the seventh chapter means anything, it means *first*, that of each kind of clean beasts, fourteen were to be taken, seven males, and seven females; *second*, that of unclean beasts should be taken, two of each kind, one of each sex, and *third*, that he should take of every kind of fowls, seven of each sex.

It is equally clear that the command in the 19th and 20th verses of the 6th chapter, is to take two of each sort, one male and one female. And this agrees exactly with the account in the 7th, 8th, 9th, 14th, 15th, and 16th verses of the 7th chapter.

The next question is, how many beasts, fowls and creeping things did Noah take into the ark?

There are now known and classified at least twelve thousand five hundred species of birds. There are still vast territories in China, South America, and Africa unknown to the ornithologist.

Of the birds, Noah took fourteen of each species, according to the 3d verse of the 7th chapter, " Of fowls also of the air by sevens, the male and the female," making a total of 175,000 birds.

And right here allow me to ask a question. If the flood was simply a partial flood, why were birds taken into the ark? It seems to me that most birds, attending strictly to business, might avoid a partial flood.

There are at least sixteen hundred and fifty-eight kinds of beasts. Let us suppose that twenty-five of these are clean. Of the clean, fourteen of each kind —seven of each sex—were taken. These amount to 350. Of the unclean—two of each kind, amounting to 3,266. There are some six hundred and fifty species of reptiles. Two of each kind amount to 1,300. And lastly, there are of insects including the creeping things, at least one million species, so that Noah and his folks had to get of these into the ark about 2,000,000.

Animalculæ have not been taken into consideration. There are probably many hundreds of thousands of species ; many of them invisible ; and yet Noah had to pick them out by pairs. Very few people have any just conception of the trouble Noah had.

We know that there are many animals on this continent not found in the Old World. These must have been carried from here to the ark, and then brought back afterwards. Were the peccary, armadillo, ant-eater, sloth, agouti, vampire-bat, marmoset, howling and prehensile-tailed monkey, the raccoon and muskrat carried by the angels from America to Asia? How did they get there? Did the polar bear leave his field of ice and journey toward the tropics? How did he know where the ark was? Did the kangaroo swim or jump from Australia to Asia? Did the giraffe, hippopotamus, antelope and orang-outang journey from Africa in search of the ark? Can absurdities go farther than this?

What had these animals to eat while on the journey? What did they eat while in the ark? What did they drink? When the rain came, of course the rivers ran to the seas, and these seas rose and finally covered the world. The waters of the seas, mingled with those of the flood, would make all salt. It has been calculated that it required, to drown the world, about eight times as much water as was in all the seas. To find how salt the waters of the flood must have been, take eight quarts of fresh water, and add one quart from the sea. Such water would create instead of allaying thirst. Noah had to take in his ark fresh water for all his beasts, birds and living things. He had to take the proper food for all. How long was he in the ark? Three hundred and seventy-seven days! Think of the food necessary for the monsters of the ante-diluvian world!

Eight persons did all the work. They attended to the wants of 175,000 birds, 3,616 beasts, 1,300 reptiles, and 2,000,000 insects, saying nothing of countless animalculæ.

Well, after they all got in, Noah pulled down the window, God shut the door, and the rain commenced.

How long did it rain?

Forty days.

How deep did the water get?

About five miles and a half.

How much did it rain a day?

Enough to cover the whole world to a depth of about seven hundred and forty-two feet.

Some Christians say that the fountains of the great deep were broken up. Will they be kind enough to tell us what the fountains of the great deep are? Others say that God had vast stores of water in the center of the earth that he used on that occasion. How did these waters happen to run up hill?

Gentlemen, allow me to tell you once more that you must not try to explain these things. Your efforts in that direction do no good, because your explanations are harder to believe than the miracle itself. Take my advice, stick to assertion, and let explanation alone.

Then, as now, Dhawalagiri lifted its crown of snow twenty-nine thousand feet above the level of the sea, and on the cloudless cliffs of Chimborazo then, as now, sat the condor; and yet the waters rising seven hundred and twenty-six feet a day—thirty feet an hour, six inches a minute,—rose over the hills, over the volcanoes, filled the vast craters, extinguished all the fires, rose above every mountain peak until the vast world was but one shoreless sea covered with the innumerable dead.

Was this the work of the most merciful God, the father of us all? If there is a God, can there be the slightest danger of incurring his displeasure by doubting even in a reverential way, the truth of such a cruel lie? If we think that God is kinder than he really is, will our poor souls be burned for that?

How many trees can live under miles of water for a year? What became of the soil washed, scattered, dissolved, and covered with the *debris* of a world? How were the tender plants and herbs preserved? How were the animals preserved after leaving the ark? There was no grass except such as had been submerged for a year. There were no animals to be devoured by the carnivorous beasts. What became of the birds that fed on worms and insects? What became of the birds that devoured other birds?

It must be remembered that the pressure of the water when at the highest point—say twenty-nine thousand feet, would have been about eight hundred tons on each square foot. Such a pressure certainly would have destroyed nearly every vestige of vegetable life, so that when the animals came out of the ark, there was not a mouthful of food in

the wide world. How were they supported
until the world was again clothed with grass?
How were those animals taken care of that subsisted on others? Where did the bees get
honey, and the ants seeds? There was not a
creeping thing upon the whole earth; not a
breathing creature beneath the whole heavens;
not a living substance. Where did the tenants
of the ark get food?

There is but one answer, if the story is true.
The food necessary not only during the year of the
flood, but sufficient for many months afterwards, must
have been stored in the ark.

There is probably not an animal in the
world that will not, in a year, eat and drink
ten times its weight. Noah must have provided food and water for a year while in the
ark, and food for at least six months after they
got ashore. It must have required for a pair
of elephants, about one hundred and fifty tons
of food and water. A couple of mammoths
would have required about twice that amount.
Of course there were other monsters that lived
on trees; and in a year would have devoured
quite a forest.

How could eight persons have distributed this food, even if the ark had been large enough to hold it? How was the ark kept clean? We know how it was ventilated; but what was done with the filth? How were the animals watered? How were some portions of the ark heated for animals from the tropics, and others kept cool for the polar bears? How did the animals get back to their respective countries? Some had to creep back about six thousand miles, and they could only go a few feet a day. Some of the creeping things must have started for the ark just as soon as they were made, and kept up a steady jog for sixteen hundred years. Think of a couple of the slowest snails leaving a point opposite the ark and starting for the plains of Shinar, a distance of twelve thousand miles. Going at the rate of a mile a month, it would take them a thousand years. How did they get there? Polar bears must have gone several thousand miles, and so sudden a change in climate must have been exceedingly trying upon their health. How did they know the way to go? Of course, all the polar bears did not go. Only two were required. Who selected these?

Two sloths had to make the journey from South America. These creatures cannot travel to exceed three rods a day. At this rate, they would make a mile in about a hundred days. They must have gone about six thousand five hundred miles, to reach the ark. Supposing them to have traveled by a reasonably direct route, in order to complete the journey before Noah hauled in the plank, they must have started several years before the world was created. We must also consider that these sloths had to board themselves on the way, and that most of their time had to be taken up getting food and water. It is exceedingly doubtful whether a sloth could travel six thousand miles and board himself in less than three thousand years.

Volumes might be written upon the infinite absurdity of this most incredible, wicked and foolish of all the fables contained in that repository of the impossible, called the Bible. To me it is a matter of amazement, that it ever was for a moment believed by any intelligent human being.

Dr. Adam Clarke says that " the animals were brought to the ark by the power of God, and their enmities were so removed or suspended, that the lion could dwell peaceably with the lamb, and the wolf sleep happily by the side of the kid. There is no positive evidence that animal food was ever used before the flood.   Noah had the first grant of this kind."

Dr. Scott remarks, "There seems to have been a very extraordinary miracle, perhaps by the ministration of angels, in bringing two of every species to Noah, and rendering them submissive, and peaceful with each other.   Yet it seems not to have made any impression upon the hardened spectators.   The suspension of the ferocity of the savage beasts during their continuance in the ark, is generally considered as an apt figure of the change that takes place in the disposition of sinners when they enter the true church of Christ."

He believed the deluge to have been universal. In his day science had not demonstrated the absurdity of this belief, and he was not compelled to resort to some theory not found in the Bible.   He insisted that " by some vast convulsion, the very bowels of the earth were forced upwards, and rain poured down in cataracts and water-spouts, with no intermission for forty days and nights, and until in every place a universal deluge was effected.

" The presence of God was the only comfort of Noah in his dreary confinement, and in witnessing the dire devastation of the earth and its inhabitants, and especially of the human species—of his companions, his neighbors, his relatives—all those to whom he had preached, for whom he had prayed and over whom he had wept, and even of many who had helped to build the ark.

" It seems that by a peculiar providential interposition, no animal of any sort died, although they had been shut up in the ark above a year; and it does not appear that there had been any increase of them during that time.

"The Ark was flat-bottomed—square at each end—roofed like a house so that it terminated at the top in the breadth of a cubit. It was divided into many little cabins for its intended inhabitants. Pitched within and without to keep it tight and sweet, and lighted from the upper part. But it must, at first sight, be evident that so large a vessel, thus constructed, with so few persons on board, was utterly unfitted to weather out the deluge, except it was under the immediate guidance and protection of the Almighty."

Dr. Henry furnished the Christian world with the following :—

" As our bodies have in them the humors which, when God pleases, become the springs and seeds of mortal disease, so the earth had, in its bowels, those waters which, at God's command, sprung up and flooded it.

" God made the world in six days, but he was forty days in destroying it, because he is slow to anger.

" The hostilities between the animals in the ark ceased, and ravenous creatures became mild and manageable, so that the wolf lay down with the lamb, and the lion ate straw like an ox.

" God shut the door of the ark to secure Noah and to keep him safe, and because it was necessary that the door should be shut very close lest the water should break in and sink the ark, and very fast lest others might break it down.

" The waters rose so high that not only the low flat countries were deluged, but to make sure work and that none might escape, the tops of the highest mountains were overflowed fifteen cubits. That is, seven and a half yards, so that salvation was not hoped for from hills or mountains.

" Perhaps some of the people got to the top of the ark, and hoped to shift for themselves there. But either they perished there for want of food, or the dashing rain washed them off the top. Others, it may be, hoped to prevail with Noah for admission into the ark, and plead old acquaintance.

" ' Have we not eaten and drank in thy presence ? Hast thou not preached in our streets ? ' ' Yea,' said Noah, ' many a time, but to little purpose. I called but ye refused ; and now it is not in my power to help you. God has shut the door and I cannot open it.'

" We may suppose that some of those who perished in the deluge had themselves assisted Noah, or were employed by him in building the ark.

" Hitherto, man had been confined to feed only upon the products of the earth. Fruits, herbs and roots, and all sorts of greens, and milk, which was the first grant ; but the flood having perhaps washed away much of the fruits of the earth, and rendered them much less pleasant and nourishing, God enlarged the grant and allowed him to eat flesh, which perhaps man never thought of until now, that God directed him to it. Nor had he any more desire to it than the sheep has to suck blood like the wolf. But now, man is allowed to feed upon flesh as freely and safely as upon the green herb."

Such was the debasing influence of a belief in the literal truth of the Bible upon these men, that their commentaries are filled with passages utterly devoid of common sense.

Dr. Clarke speaking of the mammoth says :

" This animal, an astonishing proof of God's power, he seems to have produced merely to show what he could do.   And after suffering a few of them to propagate, he extinguished the race by a merciful providence, that they might not destroy both man and beast.

" We are told that it would have been much easier for God to destroy all the people and make new ones, but he would not want to waste anything and no power or skill should be lavished where no necessity exists.

" The animals were brought to the ark by the power of God."

Again gentlemen, let me warn you of the danger of trying to explain a miracle.   Let it alone.   Say that you do not understand it, and do not expect to until taught in the schools of the New Jerusalem. The more reasons you give, the more unreasonable the miracle will appear.   Through what you say in defence, people are led to think, and as soon as they really think, the miracle is thrown away.

Among the most ignorant nations you will find the most wonders, among the most enlightened, the least. It is with individuals, the same as with nations. Ignorance believes, Intelligence examines and explains.

For about seven months the ark, with its cargo of men, animals and insects, tossed and wandered without rudder or sail upon a boundless sea. At last it grounded on the mountains of Ararat ; and about three months afterward the tops of the mountains became visible. It must not be forgotten that the mountain where the ark is supposed to have first touched bottom, was about seventeen thousand feet high. How were the animals from the tropics kept warm ? When the waters were abated it would be intensely cold at a point seventeen thousand feet above the level of the sea. May be there were stoves, furnaces, fire places and steam coils in the ark, but they are not mentioned in the inspired narrative. How were the animals kept from freezing ? It will not do to say that Ararat was not very high after all.

If you will read the fourth and fifth verses of the eight chapter you will see that although " the ark rested in the seventh month, on the seventeenth day of the month, upon the mountains of Ararat, it was not until the first day of the tenth month "that the tops of the mountains could be seen." From this it would seem that the ark must have rested upon about the highest peak in that country. Noah waited forty days more, and then for the first time opened the window and took a breath of fresh air. He then sent out a raven that did not return, then a dove that returned. He then waited seven days and sent forth a dove that returned not. From this he knew that the waters were abated. Is it possible that he could not see whether the waters had gone? Is it possible to conceive of a more perfectly childish way of ascertaining whether the earth was dry?

At last Noah " removed the covering of the ark, and looked and behold the face of the ground was dry," and thereupon God told him to disembark. In his gratitude Noah built an altar and took of every clean beast and of every clean fowl, and offered burnt offerings. And the Lord smelled a sweet savor and said in his heart that he would not any more curse the ground for man's sake. For saying this in his heart the Lord gives as a reason, not that man is, or will be good, but because " the imagination of man's heart is evil from his youth." God destroyed man because " the wickedness of man was great in the earth, and *because every imagination of the thoughts of his heart was only evil continually.*" And he promised for the same reason not to destroy him again. Will some gentleman skilled in theology give us an explanation?

After God had smelled the sweet savor of sacrifice, he seems to have changed his idea as to the proper diet for man. When Adam and Eve were created they were allowed to eat herbs bearing seed, and the fruit of trees. When they were turned out of Eden, God said to them "Thou shalt eat the herb of the field." In the first chapter of Genesis the "green herb" was given for food to the beasts, fowls and creeping things. Upon being expelled from the garden, Adam and Eve, as to their food, were put upon an equality with the lower animals. According to this, the ante-diluvians were vegetarians. This may account for their wickedness and longevity.

After Noah sacrificed, and God smelled the sweet savor; he said—"Every moving thing that liveth shall be meat for you, even as the green herb have I given you all things." Afterward this same God changed his mind again, and divided the beasts and birds into clean and unclean, and made it a crime for man to eat the unclean. Probably food was so scarce when Noah was let out of the ark that Jehovah generously allowed him to eat anything and everything he could find.

According to the account, God then made a covenant with Noah to the effect that he would not again destroy the world with a flood, and as the attesting witness of this contract, a rainbow was set in the cloud. This bow was placed in the sky so that it might perpetually remind God of his promise and covenant. Without this visible witness and reminder, it would seem that Jehovah was liable to forget the contract, and drown the world again. Did the rainbow originate in this way? Did God put it in the cloud simply to keep his agreement in his memory?

For me it is impossible to believe the story of the deluge. It seems so cruel, so barbaric, so crude in detail, so absurd in all its parts, and so contrary to all we know of law, that even credulity itself is shocked.

Many nations have preserved accounts of a deluge in which all people, except a family or two, were destroyed. Babylon was certainly a city before Jerusalem was founded. Egypt was in the height of her power when there were only seventy Jews in the world, and India had a literature before the name of Jehovah had passed the lips of superstition. An account of a general deluge "was discovered by George Smith, translated from another account that was written about two thousand years before Christ." Of course it is impossible to tell how long the story had lived in the memory of tradition before it was reduced to writing by the Babylonians. According to this account, which is, without doubt, much older than the one given by Moses, Tamzi built a ship at the command of the god Hea, and put in it his family and the beasts of the field. He pitched the ship inside and outside with bitumen, and as soon as it was finished, there came a flood of rain and "destroyed all life from the face of the whole earth. On the seventh day there was a calm, and the ship stranded on the mountain Nizir." Tamzi waited for seven days more, and then let out a dove. Afterwards, he let out a swallow, and that, as well as the dove returned. Then he let out a raven, and as that did not return, he concluded that the water had dried away, and thereupon left the ship. Then he made an offering to god, or the gods, and " Hea interceded with Bel," so that the earth might never again be drowned.

This is the Babylonian story, told without the contradictions of the original. For in that, it seems, there are two accounts, as well as in the Bible. Is it not a strange coincidence that there should be contradictory accounts mingled in both the Babylonian and Jewish stories?

In the Bible there are two accounts. In one account, Noah was to take two of all beasts, birds, and creeping things into the ark, while in the other, he was commanded to take of clean beasts, and all birds by sevens of each kind. According to one account, the flood only lasted one hundred and fifty days—as related in the third verse of the eighth chapter; while the other account fixes the time at three hundred and seventy-seven days. Both of these accounts cannot be true. Yet in order to be saved, it is not sufficient to believe one of them — you must believe both.

Among the Egyptians there was a story to the effect that the great god Ra became utterly maddened with the people, and deliberately made up his mind that he would exterminate mankind. Thereupon he began to destroy, and continued in the terrible work until blood flowed in streams, when suddenly he ceased, and took an oath that he would not again destroy the human race.   This myth was probably thousands of years old when Moses was born.

So, in India, there was a fable about the flood. A fish warned Manu that a flood was coming. Manu built a "box" and the fish towed it to a mountain and saved all hands.

The same kind of stories were told in Greece, and among our own Indian tribes.   At one time the Christian pointed to the fact that many nations told of a flood, as evidence of the truth of the Mosaic account; but now, it having been shown that other accounts are much older, and equally reasonable, that argument has ceased to be of any great value.

It is probable that all these accounts had a common origin.   They were likely born of something in nature visible to all nations.   The idea of a universal flood, produced by a god to drown the world on account of the sins of the people, is infinitely absurd.   The solution of all these stories has been supposed to be, the existence of partial floods in most countries; and for a long time this solution was satisfactory.   But the fact that these stories are greatly alike, that only one man is warned, that only one family is saved, that a boat is built, that birds are sent out to find if the water had abated, tend to show

that they had a common origin. Admitting that
there were severe floods in all countries; it certainly
cannot follow that in each instance only one family
would be saved, or that the same story would in each
instance be told. It may be urged that the natural
tendency of man to exaggerate calamities, might
account for this agreement in all the accounts, and it
must be admitted that there is some force in the
suggestion. I believe, though, that the real origin
of all these myths is the same, and that it was
originally an effort to account for the sun, moon and
stars. The sun and moon were the man and wife,
or the god and goddess, and the stars were their
children. From a celestial myth, it became a ter-
restrial one ; the air, or ether-ocean became a flood,
produced by rain, and the sun moon and stars
became man, woman and children.

In the original story, the mountain was the place
where in the far east the sky was supposed to touch
the earth, and it was there that the ship containing
the celestial passengers finally rested from its voyage.
But whatever may be the origin of the stories of the
flood, whether told first by Hindu, Babylonian or
Hebrew, we may rest perfectly assured that they are
all equally false.

XIX.

BACCHUS AND BABEL.

As soon as Noah had disembarked, he proceeded to plant a vineyard, and began to be a husbandman ; and when the grapes were ripe he made wine and drank of it to excess ; cursed his grandson, blessed Shem and Japheth, and after that lived for three hundred and fifty years. What he did during these three hundred and fifty years, we are not told. We never hear of him again. For three hundred and fifty years he lived among his sons, and daughters, and their descendants. He must have been a venerable man. He was the man to whom God had made known his intention of drowning the world. By his efforts, the human race had been saved. He must have been acquainted with Methuselah for six hundred years, and Methuselah was about two hundred and forty years old, when Adam died. Noah must himself have known the history of mankind, and must have been an object of almost infinite interest ; and yet for three hundred and fifty years he is neither directly nor indirectly mentioned. When Noah died, Abraham must have been more than fifty years old ; and Shem, the son of Noah, lived for several hundred years after the death of Abraham ; and yet he is never mentioned. Noah when he died, was the oldest man in the whole world by about five hundred years ; and everybody living at the time of his death knew that they were indebted to him, and yet no account is given of his burial. No monument was raised to mark the spot. This, however, is no more wonderful than the fact that no account is given of the death of Adam or of Eve, nor of the place of their burial. This may all be accounted for by the fact that the language of man was confounded at the building of the tower of Babel, whereby all tradition may have been lost, so that even the sons of Noah could not give an account of their voyage in the ark ; and, consequently, some one had to be directly inspired to tell the story, after new languages had been formed.

It has always been a mystery to me how Adam, Eve, and the serpent were taught the same language. Where did they get it ? We know now, that it re-quires a great number of years to form a language ;

that it is of exceedingly slow growth. We also know that by language, man conveys to his fellows the impressions made upon him by what he sees, hears, smells and touches. We know that the language of the savage consists of a few sounds, capable of expressing only a few ideas or states of the mind, such as love, desire, fear, hatred, aversion and contempt. Many centuries are required to produce a language capable of expressing complex ideas. It does not seem to me that ideas can be manufactured by a deity and put in the brain of man. These ideas must be the result of observation and experience.

Does anybody believe that God directly taught a language to Adam and Eve, or that he so made them that they, by intuition spoke Hebrew, or some language capable of conveying to each other their thoughts? How did the serpent learn the same language? Did God teach it to him, or did he happen to overhear God, when he was teaching Adam and Eve? We are told in the second chapter of Genesis that God caused all the animals to pass before Adam to see what he would call them. We cannot infer from this that God named the animals and informed Adam what to call them. Adam

named them himself.   Where did he get his words?
We cannot imagine a man just made out of dust,
without the experience of a moment, having the
power to put his thoughts in language.   In the first
place, we cannot conceive of his having any thoughts
until he has combined, through experience and observation, the impressions that nature had made upon
him through the medium of his senses.   We cannot
imagine of his knowing anything, in the first instance,
about different degrees of heat, nor about darkness, if
he was made in the day-time, nor about light, if created at night, until the next morning.   Before a man
can have what we call thoughts, he must have had
a little experience.   Something must have happened
to him before he can have a thought, and before he
can express himself in language.   Language is a
growth, not a gift.   We account now for the
diversity of language by the fact that tribes and
nations have had different experiences, different
wants, different surroundings, and, one result of all
these differences is, among other things, a difference
in language.   Nothing can be more absurd than to
account for the different languages of the world by
saying that the original language was confounded at
the tower of Babel.

According to the Bible, up to the time of the building of that tower, the whole earth was of one language and of one speech, and would have so remained until the present time had not an effort been made to build a tower whose top should reach into heaven. Can any one imagine what objection God would have to the building of such a tower? And how could the confusion of tongues prevent its construction? How could language be confounded? It could be confounded only by the destruction of memory. Did God destroy the memory of mankind at that time, and if so, how? Did he paralyze that portion of the brain presiding over the organs of articulation, so that they could not speak the words, although they remembered them clearly, or did he so touch the brain that they could not hear? Will some theologian, versed in the machinery of the miraculous, tell us in what way God confounded the language of mankind?

Why would the confounding of the language make them separate? Why would they not stay together until they could understand each other? People will not separate, from weakness. When in trouble they come together and desire the assistance

of each other.   Why, in this instance, did they
separate ?   What particular ones would naturally
come together if nobody understood the language
of any other person ?   Would it not have been just
as hard to agree when and where to go, without any
language to express the agreement, as to go on with
the building of the tower ?

Is it possible that any one now believes that the
whole world would be of one speech had the language not been confounded at Babel ?   Do we not
know that every word was suggested in some way
by the experience of men ?   Do we not know that
words are continually dying, and continually being
born ; that every language has its cradle and its
cemetery—its buds, its blossoms, its fruits and its
withered leaves ?   Man has loved, enjoyed, hated,
suffered and hoped, and all words have been born of
these experiences.

Why did " the Lord come down to see the city
and the tower " ?   Could he not see them from
where he lived or from where he was ?   Where did
he come down from ?   Did he come in the daytime,
or in the night ?   We are taught now that God is
everywhere ; that he inhabits immensity ; that he is
in every atom, and in every star.   If this is true,

why did he "come down to see the city and the tower?" Will some theologian explain this?

After all, is it not much easier and altogether more reasonable to say that Moses was mistaken, that he knew little of the science of language, and that he guessed a great deal more than he investigated?

XX.

FAITH IN FILTH.

No light whatever is shed upon what passed in the world after the confounding of language at Babel, until the birth of Abraham. But, before speaking of the history of the Jewish people, it may be proper for me to say that many things are recounted in Genesis, and other books attributed to Moses, of which I do not wish to speak. There are many pages of these books unfit to read, many stories not calculated, in my judgment, to improve the morals of mankind. I do not wish even to call the attention of my readers to these things, except in a general way. It is to be hoped that the time will come when such chapters and passages as cannot be read without leaving the blush of shame upon the cheek of modesty, will be left out, and not published as a part of the Bible. If there is a God, it certainly is blasphemous to attribute to him the authorship of pages too obscene, beastly and vulgar to be read in the presence of men and women.

The believers in the Bible are loud in their denunciation of what they are pleased to call the immoral literature of the world ; and yet few books have been published containing more moral filth than this inspired word of God.   These stories are not redeemed by a single flash of wit or humor. They never rise above the dull details of stupid vice. For one, I cannot afford to soil my pages with extracts from them ; and all such portions of the Scriptures I leave to be examined, written upon, and explained by the clergy.   Clergymen may know some way by which they can extract honey from these flowers.   Until these passages are expunged from the Old Testament, it is not a fit book to be read by either old or young.   It contains pages that no minister in the United States would read to his congregation for any reward whatever.   There are chapters that no gentleman would read in the presence of a lady.   There are chapters that no father would read to his child.   There are narratives utterly unfit to be told ; and the time will come when mankind will wonder that such a book was ever called inspired.

I know that in many books besides the Bible, there are immodest lines. Some of the greatest writers have soiled their pages with indecent words. We account for this by saying that the authors were human ; that they catered to the taste and spirit of their times. We make excuses, but at the same time regret that in their works they left an impure word. But what shall we say of God ? Is it possible that a being of infinite purity—the author of modesty, would smirch the pages of his book with stories lewd, licentious and obscene ? If God is the author of the Bible, it is, of course, the standard by which all other books can, and should be measured. If the Bible is not obscene, what book is ? Why should men be imprisoned simply for imitating God ? The Christian world should never say another word against immoral books until it makes the inspired volume clean. These vile and filthy things were not written for the purpose of conveying and enforcing moral truth, but·seem to have been written because the author loved an unclean thing. There is no moral depth below that occupied by the writer or publisher of obscene books, that stain with lust, the loving heart of youth. Such men should be im-prisoned and their books destroyed. The literature of the world should be rendered decent, and no book should be published that cannot be read by, and in the hearing of the best and purest people. But as long as the Bible is considered as the work of God, it will be hard to make all men too good and pure to imitate it; and as long as it is imitated there will be vile and filthy books. The literature of our country will not be sweet and clean until the Bible ceases to be regarded as the production of a god.

We are continually told that the Bible is the very foundation of modesty and morality ; while many of its pages are so immodest and immoral that a minister, for reading them in the pulpit, would be instantly denounced as an unclean wretch. Every woman would leave the church, and if the men stayed, it would be for the purpose of chastising the minister.

Is there any saving grace in hypocrisy ? Will men become clean in speech by believing that God is unclean ? Would it not be far better to admit that the Bible was written by barbarians in a barbarous, coarse and vulgar age ? Would it not be safer to charge Moses with vulgarity, instead of God ? Is it not altogether more probable that some ignorant Hebrew would write the vulgar words ? The Chris·

tians tell me that God is the author of these vile and stupid things? I have examined the question to the best of my ability, and as to God my verdict is :— Not guilty. Faith should not rest in filth.

Every foolish and immodest thing should be expunged from the Bible. Let us keep the good. Let us preserve every great and splendid thought, every wise and prudent maxim, every just law, every elevated idea, and every word calculated to make man nobler and purer, and let us have the courage to throw the rest away. The souls of children should not be stained and soiled. The charming instincts of youth should not be corrupted and defiled. The girls and boys should not be taught that unclean words were uttered by "inspired" lips. Teach them that these words were born of savagery and lust. Teach them that the unclean is the unholy, and that only the pure is sacred.

XXI.

THE HEBREWS.

AFTER language had been confounded and the
people scattered, there appeared in the land
of Canaan a tribe of Hebrews ruled by a chief or
sheik called Abraham. They had a few cattle, lived
in tents, practiced polygamy, wandered from place to
place, and were the only folks in the whole world
to whom God paid the slightest attention. At this
time there were hundreds of cities in India filled with
temples and palaces ; millions of Egyptians worshiped Isis and Osiris, and had covered their land
with marvelous monuments of industry, power and
skill. But these civilizations were entirely neglected
by the Deity, his whole attention being taken up
with Abraham and his family.

It seems, from the account, that God and
Abraham were intimately acquainted, and conversed
frequently upon a great variety of subjects. By the
twelfth chapter of Genesis it appears that he made

the following promises to Abraham. " I will make
of thee a great nation, and I will bless thee, and
make thy name great : and thou shalt be a blessing.
And I will bless them that bless thee, and curse him
that curseth thee."

After receiving this communication from the
Almighty, Abraham went into the land of Canaan,
and again God appeared to him and told him to take
a heifer three years old, a goat of the same age, a
sheep of equal antiquity, a turtle dove and a young
pigeon. Whereupon Abraham killed the animals
" and divided them in the midst, and laid each piece
one against another." And it came to pass that
when the sun went down and it was dark, behold a
smoking furnace and a burning lamp that passed
between the raw and bleeding meat. The killing of
these animals was a preparation for receiving a visit
from God. Should an American missionary in
Central Africa find a negro chief surrounded by a
butchered heifer, a goat and a sheep, with which to
receive a communication from the infinite God, my
opinion is, that the missionary would regard the
proceeding as the direct result of savagery. And if
the chief insisted that he had seen a smoking furnace
and a burning lamp going up and down between the

pieces of meat, the missionary would certainly conclude that the chief was not altogether right in his
mind.

If the Bible is true, this same God told Abraham
to take and sacrifice his only son, or rather the only
son of his wife, and a murder would have been
committed had not God, just at the right moment,
directed him to stay his hand and take a sheep
instead.

God made a great number of promises to
Abraham, but few of them were ever kept. He
agreed to make him the father of a great nation, but
he did not. He solemnly promised to give him a
great country, including all the land between the
river of Egypt and the Euphrates, but he did not.

In due time Abraham passed away, and his son
Isaac took his place at the head of the tribe. Then
came Jacob, who " watered stock " and enriched
himself with the spoil of Laban. Joseph was sold
into Egypt by his jealous brethren, where he became
one of the chief men of the kingdom, and in a few
years his father and brothers left their own country
and settled in Egypt. At this time there were
seventy Hebrews in the world, counting Joseph and
his children. They remained in Egypt two hundred

and fifteen years. It is claimed by some that they were in that country for four hundred and thirty years. This is a mistake. Josephus says they were in Egypt two hundred and fifteen years, and this statement is sustained by the best biblical scholars of all denominations. According to the 17th verse of the 3rd chapter of Galatians, it was four hundred and thirty years from the time the promise was made to Abraham to the giving of the law, and as the Hebrews did not go to Egypt for two hundred and fifteen years after the making of the promise to Abraham, they could in no event have been in Egypt more than two hundred and fifteen years. In our Bible the 40th verse of the 12th chapter of Exodus, is as follows:—

"Now the sojourning of the children of Israel, who dwelt in Egypt, was four hundred and thirty years."

This passage does not say that the sojourning was all done in Egypt; neither does it say that the children of Israel dwelt in Egypt four hundred and thirty years; but it does say that the sojourning of the children of Israel who dwelt in Egypt was four hundred and thirty years. The vatican copy of the Septuagint renders the same passage as follows:—

"The sojourning of the children of Israel which they sojourned in Egypt, and in the land of Canaan, was four hundred and thirty years."

The Alexandrian version says :—"The sojourning of the children of Israel which they and their fathers sojourned in Egypt, and in the land of Canaan, was four hundred and thirty years."

And in the Samaritan Bible we have :—" The sojourning of the children of Israel and of their fathers which they sojourned in the land of Canaan, and in the land of Egypt, was four hundred and thirty years."

There were seventy souls when they went down into Egypt, and they remained two hundred and fifteen years, and at the end of that time they had increased to about three million. How do we know that there were three million at the end of two hundred and fifteen years? We know it because we are informed by Moses that "there were six hundred thousand men of war." Now, to each man of war, there must have been at least five other people. In every State in this Union there will be to each voter, five other persons at least, and we all know that there are always more voters than men of war. If there were six hundred thousand men of war, there must have been a population of at least three million. Is it possible that seventy people could increase to that extent in two hundred and fifteen years? You may say that it was a miracle; but what need was there of working a miracle? Why should God miraculously increase the number of slaves? If he wished miraculously to increase the population, why did he not wait until the people were free?

In 1776, we had in the American Colonies about three millions of people. In one hundred years we doubled four times: that is to say, six, twelve, twenty-four, forty-eight million,—our present population.

We must not forget that during all these years there has been pouring into our country a vast stream of emigration, and that this, taken in connection with the fact that our country is productive beyond all others, gave us only four doubles in one hundred years. Admitting that the Hebrews increased as rapidly without emigration as we, in this country, have with it, we will give to them four doubles each century, commencing with seventy people, and they would have, at the end of two hundred years, a population of seventeen thousand nine hundred and twenty. Giving them another double for the odd fifteen years and there would be, provided no deaths had occurred, thirty-five thousand eight hundred and forty people. And yet we are told that instead of having this number, they had increased to such an extent that they had six hundred thousand men of war ; that is to say, a population of more than three millions ?

Every sensible man knows that this account is not, and cannot be true. We know that seventy people could not increase to three million in two hundred and fifteen years.

About this time the Hebrews took a census, and found that there were twenty-two thousand two hundred and seventy-three first-born males. It is reasonable to suppose that there were about as many first-born females. This would make forty-four thousand five hundred and forty-six first-born children. Now, there must have been about as many mothers as there were first-born children. If there were only about forty-five thousand mothers and three millions of people, the mothers must have had on an average about sixty-six children apiece.

At this time, the Hebrews were slaves, and had been for two hundred and fifteen years. A little while before, an order had been made by the

Egyptians that all the male children of the Hebrews should be killed. One, contrary to this order, was saved in an ark made of bullrushes daubed with slime. This child was found by the daughter of Pharaoh, and was adopted, it seems, as her own, and, may be, was. He grew to be a man, sided with the Hebrews, killed an Egyptian that was smiting a slave, hid the body in the sand, and fled from Egypt to the land of Midian, became acquainted with a priest who had seven daughters, took the side of the daughters against the ill-mannered shep-herds of that country, and married Zipporah, one of the girls, and became a shepherd for her father. Afterward, while tending his flock, the Lord appeared to him in a burning bush, and commanded him to go to the king of Egypt and demand from him the liberation of the Hebrews. In order to convince him that the something burning in the bush was actually God, the rod in his hand was changed into a serpent, which, upon being caught by the tail, became again a rod. Moses was also told to put his hand in his bosom, and when he took it out it was as leprous as snow. Quite a number of strange things were performed, and others promised. Moses then agreed to go back to Egypt provided his

brother could go with him. Whereupon the Lord
appeared to Aaron, and directed him to meet Moses
in the wilderness. They met at the mount of God,
went to Egypt, gathered together all the elders of
the children of Israel, spake all the words which God
had spoken unto Moses, and did all the signs in the
sight of the people. The Israelites believed, bowed
their heads and worshiped; and Moses and Aaron
went in and told their message to **Pharaoh the**
king.

XXII.

THE PLAGUES.

THREE millions of people were in slavery. They were treated with the utmost rigor, and so fearful were their masters that they might, in time, increase in numbers sufficient to avenge themselves, that they took from the arms of mothers all the male children and destroyed them. If the account given is true, the Egyptians were the most cruel, heartless and infamous people of which history gives any record. God finally made up his mind to free the Hebrews ; and for the accomplishment of this purpose he sent, as his agents, Moses and Aaron, to the king of Egypt. In order that the king might know that these men had a divine mission, God gave Moses the power of changing a stick into a serpent, and water into blood. Moses and Aaron went before the king, stating that the Lord God of Israel ordered the king of Egypt to let the Hebrews go that they might hold a feast with God in the wilderness. Thereupon Pharaoh, the king, enquired who the Lord was, at the same time stating that he had never made his acquaintance, and knew nothing about him. To this they replied that the God of the Hebrews had met with them, and they asked to go a three days journey into the desert and sacrifice unto this God, fearing that if they did not he would fall upon them with pestilence or the sword. This interview seems to have hardened Pharaoh, for he ordered the tasks of the children of Israel to be increased ; so that the only effect of the first appeal was to render still worse the condition of the Hebrews. Thereupon, Moses returned unto the Lord and said, " Lord, wherefore hast thou so evil entreated this people ? Why is it that thou hast sent me ? For since I came to Pharaoh to speak in thy name he hath done evil to this people ; neither hast thou delivered thy people at all."

Apparently stung by this reproach, God answered :—

" Now shalt thou see what I will do to Pharoah ; for with a strong hand shall he let them go ; and with a strong hand shall he drive them out of his land."

God then recounts the fact that he had appeared
unto Abraham, Isaac and Jacob, that he had established a covenant with them to give them the land
of Canaan, that he had heard the groanings of the
children of Israel in Egyptian bondage ; that their
groanings had put him in mind of his covenant, and
that he had made up his mind to redeem the children
of Israel with a stretched-out arm and with great
judgments. Moses then spoke to the children of
Israel again, but they would listen to him no more.
His first effort in their behalf had simply doubled
their trouble and they seemed to have lost confidence
in his power. Thereupon Jehovah promised Moses
that he would make him a god unto Pharaoh, and
that Aaron should be his prophet, but at the same
time informed him that his message would be of no
avail ; that he would harden the heart of Pharaoh so
that he would not listen ; that he would so harden
his heart that he might have an excuse for destroying the Egyptians. Accordingly, Moses and Aaron
again went before Pharaoh. Moses said to Aaron ;
—" Cast down your rod before Pharaoh," which he
did, and it became a serpent. Then Pharaoh not in
the least surprised, called for his wise men and his
sorcerers, and they threw down their rods and

changed them into serpents. The serpent that had
been changed from Aaron's rod was, at this time
crawling upon the floor, and it proceeded to swallow
the serpents that had been produced by the
magicians of Egypt. What became of these serpents
that were swallowed, whether they turned back into
sticks again, is not stated. Can we believe that the
stick was changed into a real living serpent, or did
it assume simply the appearance of a serpent? If it
bore only the appearance of a serpent it was a
deception, and could not rise above the dignity of
legerdemain. Is it necessary to believe that God
is a kind of prestigiator—a sleight-of-hand performer, a magician or sorcerer? Can it be possible
that an infinite being would endeavor to secure the
liberation of a race by performing a miracle that
could be equally performed by the sorcerers and
magicians of a barbarian king?

Not one word was said by Moses or Aaron as to
the wickedness of depriving a human being of his
liberty. Not a word was said in favor of liberty.
Not the slightest intimation that a human being was
justly entitled to the product of his own labor. Not
a word about the cruelty of masters who would
destroy even the babes of slave mothers. It seems

to me wonderful that this God did not tell the king
of Egypt that no nation could enslave another, without also enslaving itself; that it was impossible to
put a chain around the limbs of a slave, without
putting manacles upon the brain of the master.
Why did he not tell him that a nation founded upon
slavery could not stand? Instead of declaring these
things, instead of appealing to justice, to mercy and
to liberty, he resorted to feats of jugglery. Suppose
we wished to make a treaty with a barbarous nation,
and the President should employ a sleight-of-hand
performer as envoy extraordinary, and instruct him,
that when he came into the presence of the savage
monarch, he should cast down an umbrella or a
walking stick, which would change into a lizard or
a turtle; what would we think? Would we not
regard such a performance as beneath the dignity
even of a President? And what would be our
feelings if the savage king sent for his sorcerers and
had them perform the same feat? If such things
would appear puerile and foolish in the President of
a great republic, what shall be said when they were
resorted to by the creator of all worlds? How
small, how contemptible such a God appears!
Pharaoh, it seems, took about this view of the

matter, and he would not be persuaded that such
tricks were performed by an infinite being.

Again, Moses and Aaron came before Pharaoh
as he was going to the river's bank, and the same
rod which had changed to a serpent, and, by this
time changed back, was taken by Aaron, who, in the
presence of Pharaoh, smote the water of the river,
which was immediately turned to blood, as well as
all the water in all the streams, ponds, and pools,
as well as all water in vessels of wood and vessels of
stone in the entire land of Egypt.   As soon as all
the waters in Egypt had been turned into blood, the
magicians of that country did the same with their
enchantments.   We are not informed where they
got the water to turn into blood, since all the water
in Egypt had already been so changed.   It seems
from the account that the fish in the Nile died, and
the river emitted a stench, and there was not a drop
of water in the land of Egypt that had not been
changed into blood.   In consequence of this, the
Egyptians digged "around about the river" for
water to drink.   Can we believe this story?   Is it
necessary to salvation to admit that all the rivers,
pools, ponds and lakes of a country were changed
into blood, in order that a king might be induced to

allow the children of Israel the privilege of going a three days journey into the wilderness to make sacrifices to their God?

It seems from the account that Pharaoh was told that the God of the Hebrews would, if he refused to let the Israelites go, change all the waters of Egypt into blood, and that, upon his refusal, they were so changed. This had, however, no influence upon him, for the reason that his own magicians did the same. It does not appear that Moses and Aaron expressed the least surprise at the success of the Egyptian sorcerers. At that time it was believed that each nation had its own god. The only claim that Moses and Aaron made for their God was, that he was the greatest and most powerful of all the gods, and that with anything like an equal chance he could vanquish the deity of any other nation.

After the waters were changed to blood Moses and Aaron waited for seven days. At the end of that time God told Moses to again go to Pharaoh and demand the release of his people, and to inform him that, if he refused, God would strike all the borders of Egypt with frogs. That he would make frogs so plentiful that they would go into the houses of Pharaoh, into his bedchamber, upon his bed, into

the houses of his servants, upon his people, into
their ovens, and even into their kneading troughs.
This threat had no effect whatever upon Pharaoh.
And thereupon Aaron stretched out his hand over
the waters of Egypt, and the frogs came up and
covered the land. The magicians of Egypt did the
same, and with their enchantments brought more
frogs upon the land of Egypt.

These magicians do not seem to have been
original in their ideas, but so far as imitation is con-
cerned, were perfect masters of their art. The frogs
seem to have made such an impression upon Pharaoh
that he sent for Moses and asked him to entreat the
Lord that he would take away the frogs. Moses
agreed to remove them from the houses and the
land, and allow them to remain only in the rivers.
Accordingly the frogs died out of the houses, and out
of the villages, and out of the fields, and the people
gathered them together in heaps. As soon as the
frogs had left the houses and fields, the heart of
Pharaoh became again hardened, and he refused to
let the people go.

Aaron then, according to the command of God,
stretched out his hand, holding the rod, and smote
the dust of the earth, and it became lice in man and

in beast, and all the dust became lice throughout the land of Egypt. Pharaoh again sent for his magicians, and they sought to do the same with their enchantments, but they could not. Whereupon the sorcerers said unto Pharaoh : " This is the finger of God."

Notwithstanding this, however, Pharaoh refused to let the Hebrews go. God then caused a grievous swarm of flies to come into the house of Pharaoh and into his servants' houses, and into all the land of Egypt, to such an extent that the whole land was corrupted by reason of the flies. But into that part of the country occupied by the children of Israel there came no flies. Thereupon Pharaoh sent for Moses and Aaron and said to them : " Go, and sacrifice to your God in this land." They were not willing to sacrifice in Egypt, and asked permission to go on a journey of three days into the wilderness. To this Pharaoh acceded, and in consideration of this Moses agreed to use his influence with the Lord to induce him to send the flies out of the country. He accordingly told the Lord of the bargain he had made with Pharaoh, and the Lord agreed to the compromise, and removed the flies from Pharaoh and from his servants and from his people, and there

remained not a single fly in the land of Egypt.   As
soon as the flies were gone, Pharaoh again changed
his mind, and concluded not to permit the children of
Israel to depart.   The Lord then directed Moses to
go to Pharaoh and tell him that if he did not allow
the children of Israel to depart, he would destroy his
cattle, his horses, his camels and his sheep ; that
these animals would be afflicted with a grievous
disease, but that the animals belonging to the
Hebrews should not be so afflicted.   Moses did as
he was bid.   On the next day all the cattle of Egypt
died ; that is to say, all the horses, all the asses, all
the camels, all the oxen and all the sheep ; but of
the animals owned by the Israelites, not one perished.
This disaster had no effect upon Pharaoh, and he still
refused to let the children of Israel go.   The Lord
then told Moses and Aaron to take some ashes
out of a furnace, and told Moses to· sprinkle them
toward the heavens in the sight of Pharaoh ; saying
that the ashes should become small dust in all the
land of Egypt, and should be a boil breaking forth
with blains upon man and upon beast throughout all
the land.

How these boils breaking out with blains, upon
cattle that were already dead, should affect Pharaoh,

is a little hard to understand. It must not be forgotten that all the cattle and all beasts had died with
the murrain before the boils had broken out.

This was a most decisive victory for Moses and
Aaron. The boils were upon the magicians to that
extent that they could not stand before Moses. But
it had no effect upon Pharaoh, who seems to have
been a man of great firmness. The Lord then
instructed Moses to get up early in the morning and
tell Pharaoh that he would stretch out his hand and
smite his people with a pestilence, and would, on the
morrow, cause it to rain a very grievous hail, such
as had never been known in the land of Egypt. He
also told Moses to give notice, so that they might
get all the cattle that were in the fields under cover.
It must be remembered that all these cattle had
recently died of the murrain, and their dead bodies
had been covered with boils and blains. This,
however, had no effect, and Moses stretched forth
his hand toward heaven, and the Lord sent thunder,
and hail and lightning, and fire that ran along the
ground, and the hail fell upon all the land of Egypt,
and all that were in the fields, both man and
beast, were smitten, and the hail smote every
herb of the field, and broke every tree of the

country except that portion inhabited by the children of Israel; there, there was no hail.

During this hail storm Pharaoh sent for Moses and Aaron and admitted that he had sinned, that the Lord was righteous, and that the Egyptians were wicked, and requested them to ask the Lord that there be no more thunderings and hail, and that he would let the Hebrews go. Moses agreed that as soon as he got out of the city he would stretch forth his hands unto the Lord, and that the thunderings should cease and the hail should stop. But, when the rain and the hail and the thundering ceased, Pharaoh concluded that he would not let the children of Israel go.

Again, God sent Moses and Aaron, instructing them to tell Pharaoh that if he refused to let the people go, the face of the earth would be covered with locusts, so that man would not be able to see the ground, and that these locusts would eat the residue of that which escaped from the hail; that they would eat every tree out of the field; that they would fill the houses of Pharaoh and the houses of all his servants, and the houses of all the Egyptians. Moses delivered the message, and went out from Pharaoh. Some of Pharaoh's servants entreated

their master to let the children of Israel go.
Pharaoh sent for Moses and Aaron and asked
them, who wished to go into the wilderness to
sacrifice. They replied that they wished to go with
the young and old ; with their sons and daughters,
with flocks and herds. Pharaoh would not consent
to this, but agreed that the men might go. Thereupon Pharaoh drove Moses and Aaron out of his
sight. Then God told Moses to stretch forth his
hand upon the land of Egypt for the locusts, that
they might come up and eat every herb, even all
that the hail had left. "And Moses stretched out
his rod over the land of Egypt, and the Lord brought
an east wind all that day and all that night ; and
when it was morning the east wind brought the
locusts ; and they came up over all the land of Egypt
and rested upon all the coasts covering the face of
the whole earth, so that the land was darkened ;
and they ate every herb and all the fruit of the
trees which the hail had left, and there remained
not any green thing on the trees or in the herbs
of the field throughout the land of Egypt." Pharaoh
then called for Moses and Aaron in great haste,
admitted that he had sinned against the Lord their
God and against them, asked their forgiveness and

requested them to intercede with God that he might
take away the locusts. They went out from his
presence and asked the Lord to drive the locusts
away, "And the Lord made a strong west wind
which took away the locusts, and cast them into the
Red Sea so that there remained not one locust in all
the coasts of Egypt."

As soon as the locusts were gone, Pharaoh
changed his mind, and, in the language of the sacred
text, "the Lord hardened Pharaoh's heart so that he
would not let the children of Israel go."

The Lord then told Moses to stretch out his
hand toward heaven that there might be darkness
over the land of Egypt, "even darkness which might
be felt." "And Moses stretched forth his hand
toward heaven, and there was a thick darkness over
the land of Egypt for three days during which time
they saw not each other, neither arose any of the
people from their places for three days; but the
children of Israel had light in their dwellings."

It strikes me that when the land of Egypt was
covered with thick darkness—so thick that it could
be felt, and when light was in the dwellings of the
Israelites, there could have been no better time for
the Hebrews to have left the country.

Pharaoh again called for Moses, and told him that his people could go and serve the Lord, provided they would leave their flocks and herds. Moses would not agree to this, for the reason that they needed the flocks and herds for sacrifices and burnt offerings, and he did not know how many of the animals God might require, and for that reason he could not leave a single hoof.   Upon the question of the cattle, they divided, and Pharaoh again refused to let the people go.   God then commanded Moses to tell the Hebrews to borrow, each of his neighbor, jewels of silver and gold.   By a miraculous interposition the Hebrews found favor in the sight of the Egyptians so that they loaned the articles asked for. After this, Moses again went to Pharaoh and told him that all the first-born in the land of Egypt, from the first-born of Pharaoh upon the throne, unto the first-born of the maid-servant who was behind the mill, as well as the first-born of beasts, should die.

As all the beasts had been destroyed by disease and hail, it is troublesome to understand the meaning of the threat as to their first-born.

Preparations were accordingly made for carrying this frightful threat into execution.   Blood was put on the door-posts of all houses inhabited by Hebrews, so that God, as he passed through that land, might not be mistaken and destroy the first-born of the Jews. " And it came to pass that at midnight the Lord smote all the first-born in the land of Egypt the first-born of Pharaoh who sat on the throne, and the first-born of the captive who was in the dungeon. And Pharaoh rose up in the night, and all his servants, and all the Egyptians, and there was a great cry in Egypt, for there was not a house where there was not one dead."

What had these children done? Why should the babes in the cradle be destroyed on account of the crime of Pharaoh? Why should the cattle be destroyed because man had enslaved his brother? In those days women and children and cattle were put upon an exact equality, and all considered as the property of the men; and when man in some way excited the wrath of God, he punished them by destroying all their cattle, their wives, and their little ones. Where can words be found bitter enough to describe a god who would kill wives and babes because husbands and fathers had failed to keep his law? Every good man, and every good woman, must hate and despise such a deity.

Upon the death of all the first-born Pharaoh sent for Moses and Aaron, and not only gave his consent that they might go with the Hebrews into the wilderness, but besought them to go at once.

Is it possible that an infinite God, creator of all worlds and sustainer of all life, said to Pharaoh, "If you do not let my people go, I will turn all the water of your country into blood," and that upon the refusal of Pharaoh to release the people, God did turn all the waters into blood? Do you believe this?

Do you believe that Pharaoh even after all the water was turned to blood, refused to let the Hebrews go, and that thereupon God told him he would cover his land with frogs? Do you believe this?

Do you believe that after the land was covered with frogs Pharaoh still refused to let the people go, and that God then said to him, "I will cover you and all your people with lice?" Do you believe God would make this threat?

Do you also believe that God told Pharaoh, "If you do not let these people go, I will fill all your houses and cover your country with flies?" Do you believe God makes such threats as this?

Of course God must have known that turning the waters into blood, covering the country with frogs, infesting all flesh with lice, and filling all houses with flies, would not accomplish his object, and that all these plagues would have no effect whatever upon the Egyptian king.

Do you believe that, failing to accomplish anything by the flies, God told Pharaoh that if he did not let the people go he would kill his cattle with murrain? Does such a threat sound God-like?

Do you believe that, failing to effect anything by killing the cattle, this same God then threatened to afflict all the people with boils, including the magicians who had been rivaling him in the matter of miracles; and failing to do anything by boils, that he resorted to hail? Does this sound reasonable? The hail experiment having accomplished nothing, do you believe that God murdered the first-born of animals and men? Is it possible to conceive of anything more utterly absurd, stupid, revolting, cruel and senseless, than the miracles said to have been wrought by the Almighty for the purpose of inducing Pharaoh to liberate the children of Israel?

Is it not altogether more reasonable to say that the Jewish people, being in slavery, accounted for

the misfortunes and calamities, suffered by the
Egyptians, by saying that they were the judgments
of God ?

When the Armada of Spain was wrecked and
scattered by the storm, the English people believed
that God had interposed in their behalf, and publicly
gave thanks.   When the battle of Lepanto was won,
it was believed by the Catholic world that the victory
was given in answer to prayer.   So, our fore-fathers
in their Revolutionary struggle saw, or thought they
saw, the hand of God, and most firmly believed that
they achieved their independence by the interposition of the Most High.

Now, it may be that while the Hebrews were
enslaved by the Egyptians, there were plagues of
locusts and flies.   It may be that there were some dis-
eases by which many of the cattle perished.   It may be
that a pestilence visited that country so that in nearly
every house there was some one dead.   If so, it was
but natural for the enslaved and superstitious Jews
to account for these calamities by saying that they
were punishments sent by their God.   Such ideas
will be found in the history of every country.

For a long time the Jews held these opinions,
and they were handed from father to son simply by

tradition. By the time a written language had been produced, thousands of additions had been made, and numberless details invented; so that we have not only an account of the plagues suffered by the Egyptians, but the whole woven into a connected story, containing the threats made by Moses and Aaron, the miracles wrought by them, the promises of Pharaoh, and finally the release of the Hebrews, as a result of the marvelous things performed in their behalf by Jehovah.

In any event it is infinitely more probable that the author was misinformed, than that the God of this universe was guilty of these childish, heartless and infamous things. The solution of the whole matter is this:—Moses was mistaken.

XXIII.

THE FLIGHT.

THREE millions of people, with their flocks and herds, with borrowed jewelry and raiment, with unleavened dough in kneading troughs bound in their clothes upon their shoulders, in one night commenced their journey for the land of promise. We are not told how they were informed of the precise time to start. With all the modern appliances, it would require months of time to inform three millions of people of any fact.

In this vast assemblage there were six hundred thousand men of war, and with them were the old, the young, the diseased and helpless. Where were those people going? They were going to the desert of Sinai, compared with which Sahara is a garden. Imagine an ocean of lava torn by storm and vexed by tempest, suddenly gazed at by a Gorgon and changed instantly to stone! Such was the desert of Sinai.

All of the civilized nations of the world could not feed and support three millions of people on the desert of Sinai for forty years. It would cost more than one hundred thousand millions of dollars, and would bankrupt Christendom. They had with them their flocks and herds, and the sheep were so numerous that the Israelites sacrificed, at one time, more than one hundred and fifty thousand first-born lambs. How were these flocks supported ? What did they eat ? Where were meadows and pastures for them ? There was no grass, no forests— nothing ! There is no account of its having rained baled hay, nor is it even claimed that they were miraculously fed. To support these flocks, millions of acres of pasture would have been required. God did not take the Israelites through the land of the Philistines, for fear that when they saw the people of that country they would return to Egypt, but he took them by the way of the wilderness to the Red Sea, going before them by day in a pillar of cloud, and by night, in a pillar of fire.

When it was told Pharaoh that the people had fled, he made ready and took six hundred chosen

chariots of Egypt, and pursued after the children of
Israel, overtaking them by the sea. As all the
animals had long before that time been destroyed,
we are not informed where Pharaoh obtained the
horses for his chariots. The moment the children
of Israel saw the hosts of Pharaoh, although they
had six hundred thousand men of war, they immediately cried unto the Lord for protection. It is
wonderful to me that a land that had been ravaged
by the plagues described in the Bible, still had the
power to put in the field an army that would carry
terror to the hearts of six hundred thousand men of
war. Even with the help of God, it seems, they were
not strong enough to meet the Egyptians in the open
field, but resorted to strategy. Moses again stretched
forth his wonderful rod over the waters of the Red
Sea, and they were divided, and the Hebrews passed
through on dry land, the waters standing up like a
wall on either side. The Egyptians pursued them ;
" and in the morning watch the Lord looked into the
hosts of the Egyptians, through the pillar of fire,"
and proceeded to take the wheels off their chariots.
As soon as the wheels were off, God told Moses to
stretch out his hand over the sea. Moses did so,
and immediately " the waters returned and covered

the chariots and horsemen and all the hosts of
Pharaoh that came into the sea, and there remained
not so much as one of them."

This account may be true, but still it hardly looks
reasonable that God would take the wheels off the
chariots. How did he do it? Did he pull out the
linch-pins, or did he just take them off by main
force?

What a picture this presents to the mind! God
the creator of the universe, maker of every shining,
glittering star, engaged in pulling off the wheels of
wagons, that he might convince Pharaoh of his
greatness and power!

Where were these people going? They were
going to the promised land. How large a country
was that? About twelve thousand square miles.
About one-fifth the size of the State of Illinois. It
was a frightful country, covered with rocks and deso-
lation. How many people were in the promised land
already? Moses tells us there were seven nations in
that country mightier than the Jews. As there were
at least three millions of Jews, there must have been
at least twenty-one millions of people already in that
country. These had to be driven out in order that
room might be made for the chosen people of God.

It seems, however, that God was not willing to take the children of Israel into the promised land immediately. They were not fit to inhabit the land of Canaan ; so he made up his mind to allow them to wander upon the desert until all except two, who had left Egypt, should perish. Of all the slaves released from Egyptian bondage, only two were allowed to reach the promised land!

As soon as the Hebrews crossed the Red Sea, they found themselves without food, and with water unfit to drink by reason of its bitterness, and they began to murmur against Moses, who cried unto the Lord, and "the Lord showed him a tree." Moses cast this tree into the waters, and they became sweet. "And it came to pass in the morning the dew lay around about the camp ; and when the dew that lay was gone, behold, upon the face of the wilderness lay a small round thing, small as the hoar-frost upon the ground. And Moses said unto them, this is the bread which the Lord hath given you to eat." This manna was a very peculiar thing. It would melt in the sun, and yet they could cook it by seething and baking. One would as soon think of frying snow or of broiling icicles. But this manna had another remarkable quality. No matter how much or little any person gathered, he would have an exact omer; if he gathered more, it would shrink to that amount, and if he gathered less, it would swell exactly to that amount. What a magnificent substance manna would be with which to make a currency—shrinking and swelling according to the great laws of supply and demand!

"Upon this manna the children of Israel lived for forty years, until they came to a habitable land. With this meat were they fed until they reached the borders of the land of Canaan." We are told in the twenty-first chapter of Numbers, that the people at last became tired of the manna, complained of God, and asked Moses why he brought them out of the land of Egypt to die in the wilderness. And they said:—"There is no bread, nor have we any water. Our soul loatheth this light food."

We are told by some commentators that the Jews lived on manna for forty years; by others that they lived upon it for only a short time. As a matter of fact the accounts differ, and this difference is the opportunity for commentators. It also allows us to exercise faith in believing that both accounts

are true.   If the accounts agreed, and were reasonable, they would be believed by the wicked and
unregenerated.   But as they are different and
unreasonable, they are believed only by the good.
Whenever a statement in the Bible is unreasonable,
and you believe it, you are considered quite a good
Christian.   If the statement is grossly absurd and
infinitely impossible, and you still believe it, you are
a saint.

The children of Israel were in the desert, and
they were out of water.   They had nothing to eat
but manna, and this they had had so long that the
soul of every person abhorred it.   Under these
circumstances they complained to Moses.   Now, as
God is infinite, he could just as well have furnished
them with an abundance of the purest and coolest of
water, and could, without the slightest trouble to
himself, have given them three excellent meals a
day, with a generous variety of meats and vegetables,
it is very hard to see why he did not do so.   It is
still harder to conceive why he fell into a rage when
the people mildly suggested that they would like a
change of diet.   Day after day, week after week,
month after month, year after year, nothing but
manna.   No doubt they did the best they could by

cooking it in different ways, but in spite of themselves they began to loathe its sight and taste, and
so they asked Moses to use his influence to secure a
change in the bill of fare.

Now, I ask, whether it was unreasonable for the
Jews to suggest that a little meat would be very
gratefully received?   It seems, however, that as
soon as the request was made, this God of infinite
mercy became infinitely enraged, and instead of
granting it, went into partnership with serpents, for
the purpose of punishing the hungry wretches to
whom he had promised a land flowing with milk
and honey.

Where did these serpents come from ?   How did
God convey the information to the serpents, that he
wished them to go to the desert of Sinai and bite
some Jews ?   It may be urged that these serpents
were created for the express purpose of punishing
the children of Israel for having had the presumption,
like Oliver Twist, to ask for more.

There is another account in the eleventh chapter
of Numbers, of the people murmuring because of their
food.   They remembered the fish, the cucumbers,
the melons, the leeks, the onions and the garlic of
Egypt, and they asked for meat.   The people went

to the tent of Moses and asked him for flesh.   Moses
cried unto the Lord and asked him why he did not
take care of the multitude.   God thereupon agreed
that they should have meat, not for a day or two,
but for a month, until the meat should come out of
their nostrils and become loathsome to them.   He
then caused a wind to bring quails from beyond the
sea, and cast them into the camp, on every side of
the camp around about for the space of a days
journey.   And the people gathered them, and while
the flesh was yet between their teeth the wrath of
God being provoked against them, struck them with
an exceeding great plague.   Serpents, also, were
sent among them, and thousands perished for the
crime of having been hungry.

The Rev. Alexander Cruden commenting upon
this account says :—

" God caused a wind to rise that drove the quails
within and about the camp of the Israelites ; and it
is in this that the miracle consists, that they were
brought so seasonably to this place, and in so great
numbers as to suffice above a million of persons
above a month.   Some authors affirm, that in those
eastern and southern countries, quails are innumerable, so that in one part of Italy within the compass

of five miles, there were taken about an hundred
thousand of them every day for a month together ;
and that sometimes they fly so thick over the sea,
that being weary they fall into ships, sometimes in
such numbers, that they sink them with their
weight."

No wonder Mr. Cruden believed the Mosaic
account.

Must we believe that God made an arrangement
with hornets for the purpose of securing their services
in driving the Canaanites from the land of promise ?
Is this belief necessary unto salvation ?   Must we
believe that God said to the Jews that he would send
hornets before them to drive out the Canaanites, as
related in the twenty-third chapter of Exodus, and
the second chapter of Deuteronomy ?   How would
the hornets know a Canaanite ?   In what way would
God put it in the mind of a hornet to attack a
Canaanite ?   Did God create hornets for that especial
purpose, implanting an instinct to attack a Canaanite,
but not a Hebrew ?   Can we conceive of the
Almighty granting letters of marque and reprisal to
hornets ?   Of course it is admitted that nothing in
the world would be better calculated to make a man
leave his native land than a few hornets.   Is it

possible for us to believe that an infinite being would
resort to such expedients in order to drive the
Canaanites from their country ?   He could just as
easily have spoken the Canaanites out of existence
as to have spoken the hornets in.   In this way a vast
amount of trouble, pain and suffering would have
been saved.   Is it possible that there is, in this
country, an intelligent clergyman who will insist that
these stories are true ; that we must believe them in
in order to be good people in this world, and glorified souls in the next ?

We are also told that God instructed the Hebrews
to kill the Canaanites slowly, giving as a reason that
the beasts of the field might increase upon his chosen
people.   When we take into consideration the fact
that the Holy Land contained only about eleven or
twelve thousand square miles, and was at that time
inhabited by at least twenty-one millions of people,
it does not seem reasonable that the wild beasts could
have been numerous enough to cause any great
alarm.   The same ratio of population would give to
the State of Illinois at least one hundred and twenty
millions of inhabitants.   Can anybody believe that,
under such circumstances, the danger from wild
beasts could be very great ?   What would we think

of a general, invading such a State, if he should order his soldiers to kill the people slowly, lest the wild beasts might increase upon them? Is it possible that a God capable of doing the miracles recounted in the Old Testament could not, in some way, have disposed of the wild beasts? After the Canaanites were driven out, could he not have employed the hornets to drive out the wild beasts? Think of a God that could drive twenty-one millions of people out of the promised land, could raise up innumerable stinging flies, and could cover the earth with fiery serpents, and yet seems to have been perfectly powerless against the wild beasts of the land of Canaan!

Speaking of these hornets, one of the good old commentators, whose views have long been considered of great value by the believers in the inspiration of the Bible, uses the following language: —" Hornets are a sort of strong flies, which the Lord used as instruments to plague the enemies of his people. They are of themselves very troublesome and mischievous, and those the Lord made use of were, it is thought, of an extraordinary bigness and perniciousness. It is said they live as the wasps, and that they have a king or captain, and pestilent

stings as bees, and that, if twenty-seven of them
sting man or beast, it is certain death to either.
Nor is it strange that such creatures did drive out
the Canaanites from their habitations ; for many
heathen writers give instances of some people driven
from their seats by frogs, others by mice, others by
bees and wasps.   And it is said that a Christian city,
being besieged by Sapores, king of Persia, was
delivered by hornets ; for the elephants and beasts
being stung by them, waxed unruly, and so the
whole army fled."

Only a few years ago, all such stories were
believed by the Christian world ; and it is a historical
fact, that Voltaire was the third man of any note in
Europe, who took the ground that the mythologies
of Greece and Rome were without foundation.
Until his time, most Christians believed as thoroughly
in the miracles ascribed to the Greek and Roman
gods as in those of Christ and Jehovah.   The
Christian world cultivated credulity, not only as one
of the virtues, but as the greatest of them all.   But,
when Luther and his followers left the Church of
Rome, they were compelled to deny the power of
the Catholic Church, at that time, to suspend the
laws of nature, but took the ground that such power

ceased with the apostolic age. They insisted that all things now happened in accordance with the laws of nature, with the exception of a few special interferences in favor of the Protestant Church in answer to prayer. They taught their children a double philosophy : by one, they were to show the impossibility of Catholic miracles, because opposed to the laws of nature ; by the other, the probability of the miracles of the apostolic age, because they were in conformity with the statements of the Scriptures. They had two foundations : one, the law of nature, and the other, the word of God. The Protestants have endeavored to carry on this double process of reasoning, and the result has been a gradual increase of confidence in the law of nature, and a gradual decrease of confidence in the word of God.

We are told, in this inspired account, that the clothing of the Jewish people did not wax old, and that their shoes refused to wear out. Some commentators have insisted that angels attended to the wardrobes of the Hebrews, patched their garments, and mended their shoes. Certain it is, however, that the same clothes lasted them for forty years, during the entire journey from Egypt to the Holy Land. Little boys starting out with their first pantaloons, grew as they traveled, and their clothes grew with them.

Can it be necessary to believe a story like this? Will men make better husbands, fathers, neighbors, and citizens, simply by giving credence to these childish and impossible things? Certainly an infinite God could have transported the Jews to the Holy Land in a moment, and could, as easily, have removed the Canaanites to some other country. Surely there was no necessity for doing thousands and thousands of petty miracles, day after day for forty years, looking after the clothes of three millions of people, changing the nature of wool and linen and leather, so that they would not "wax old." Every step, every motion, would wear away some part of the clothing, some part of the shoes. Were these parts, so worn away, perpetually renewed, or was the nature of things so changed that they could not wear away? We know that whenever matter comes in contact with matter, certain atoms, by abrasion, are lost. Were these atoms gathered up every night by angels, and replaced on the soles of the shoes, on the elbows of coats, and on the knees of pantaloons, so that the next morning they would be precisely in the condition they were on the morning before ? There must be a mistake somewhere.

Can we believe that the real God, if there is one, ever ordered a man to be killed simply for making hair oil, or ointment? We are told in the thirtieth chapter of Exodus, that the Lord commanded Moses to take myrrh, cinnamon, sweet calamus, cassia, and olive oil, and make a holy ointment for the purpose of anointing the tabernacle, tables, candlesticks and other utensils, as well as Aaron and his sons ; saying, at the same time, that whosoever compounded any like it, or whoever put any of it on a stranger, should be put to death. In the same chapter, the Lord furnishes Moses with a recipe for making a perfume, saying, that whoever should make any which smelled like it, should be cut off from his people. This, to me, sounds so unreasonable that I cannot believe it. Why should an infinite God care whether mankind made ointments and perfumes like his or not ? Why should the Creator of all things threaten to kill a priest who approached his altar without having washed his hands and feet ? These commandments and these penalties would disgrace the vainest tyrant that ever sat, by chance, upon a throne. There must be some mistake. I cannot

believe that an infinite Intelligence appeared to
Moses upon Mount Sinai having with him a variety
of patterns for making a tabernacle, tongs, snuffers
and dishes.   Neither can I believe that God told
Moses how to cut and trim a coat for a priest.   Why
should a God care about such things ?   Why should
he insist on having buttons sewed in certain rows,
and fringes of a certain color ?   Suppose an intelligent civilized man was to overhear, on Mount Sinai,
the following instructions from God to Moses :—

" You must consecrate my priests as follows :—
You must kill a bullock for a sin offering, and
have Aaron and his sons lay their hands upon the
head of the bullock.   Then you must take the blood
and put it upon the horns of the altar round about
with your finger, and pour some blood at the bottom
of the altar to make a reconciliation ; and of the fat
that is upon the inwards, the caul above the liver
and two kidneys, and their fat, and burn them upon
the altar.   You must get a ram for a burnt offering,
and Aaron and his sons must lay their hands upon
the head of the ram.   Then you must kill it and
sprinkle the blood upon the altar, and cut the ram
into pieces, and burn the head, and the pieces, and
the fat, and wash the inwards and the lungs in water

and then burn the whole ram upon the altar for a sweet savor unto me. Then you must get another ram, and have Aaron and his sons lay their hands upon the head of that, then kill it and take of its blood, and put it on the top of Aaron's right ear, and on the thumb of his right hand, and on the great toe of his right foot. And you must also put a little of the blood upon the top of the right ears of Aaron's sons, and on the thumbs of their right hands and on the great toes of their right feet. And then you must take of the fat that is on the inwards, and the caul above the liver and the two kidneys, and their fat, and the right shoulder, and out of a basket of unleavened bread you must take one unleavened cake and another of oil bread, and one wafer, and put them on the fat of the right shoulder. And you must take of the anointing oil, and of the blood, and sprinkle it on Aaron, and on his garments, and on his sons' garments, and sanctify them and all their clothes."—Do you believe that he would have even suspected that the creator of the universe was talking ?

Can any one now tell why God commanded the Jews, when they were upon the desert of Sinai, to plant trees, telling them at the same time that they must not eat any of the fruit of such trees until after the fourth year? Trees could not have been planted in that desert, and if they had been, they could not have lived. Why did God tell Moses, while in the desert, to make curtains of fine linen? Where could he have obtained his flax? There was no land upon which it could have been produced. Why did he tell him to make things of gold, and silver, and precious stones, when they could not have been in possession of these things? There is but one answer, and that is, the Pentateuch was written hundreds of years after the Jews had settled in the Holy Land, and hundreds of years after Moses was dust and ashes.

When the Jews had a written language, and that must have been long after their flight from Egypt, they wrote out their history and their laws. Tradition had filled the infancy of the nation with miracles and special interpositions in their behalf by Jehovah. Patriotism would not allow these wonders to grow small, and priestcraft never denied a miracle. There were traditions to the effect that God had spoken face to face with Moses; that he had given him the tables of the law, and had, in a thousand ways, made known his will; and whenever the priests wished to

make new laws, or amend old ones, they pretended
to have found something more that God said to
Moses at Sinai.   In this way obedience was more
easily secured.   Only a very few of the people could
read, and, as a consequence, additions, interpolations
and erasures had no fear of detection.   In this way
we account for the fact that Moses is made to speak
of things that did not exist in his day, and were
unknown for hundreds of years after his death.

In the thirtieth chapter of Exodus, we are told
that the people, when numbered, must give each one
a half shekel after the shekel of the *sanctuary*.   At
that time no such money existed, and consequently
the account could not, by any possibility, have been
written until after there was a shekel of the sanctuary,
and there was no such thing until long after the
death of Moses.   If we should read that Cæsar paid
his troops in pounds, shillings and pence, we would
certainly know that the account was not written by
Cæsar, nor in his time, but we would know that it
was written after the English had given these names
to certain coins.

So, we find, that when the Jews were upon the
desert it was commanded that every mother should
bring, as a sin offering, a couple of doves to the

priests, and the priests were compelled to eat these doves in the most holy place.   At the time this law appears to have been given, there were three million people, and only three priests, Aaron, Eleazer and Ithamar.   Among three million people there would be, at least, three hundred births a day.   Certainly we are not expected to believe that these three priests devoured six hundred pigeons every twenty-four hours.

Why should a woman ask pardon of God for having been a mother?   Why should that be considered a crime in Exodus, which is commanded as a duty in Genesis?   Why should a mother be declared unclean?   Why should giving birth to a daughter be regarded twice as criminal as giving birth to a son?   Can we believe that such laws and ceremonies were made and instituted by a merciful and intelligent God?   If there is anything in this poor world suggestive of, and standing for, all that is sweet, loving and pure, it is a mother holding in her thrilled and happy arms her prattling babe.   Read the twelfth chapter of Leviticus, and you will see that when a woman became the mother of a boy she was so unclean that she was not allowed to touch a hallowed thing, nor to enter the sanctuary for forty days.   If the babe was a girl, then the mother was unfit for eighty days, to enter the house of God, or to touch the sacred tongs and snuffers. These laws, born of barbarism, are unworthy of our day, and should be regarded simply as the mistakes of savages.

Just as low in the scale of intelligence are the directions given in the fifth chapter of Numbers, for the trial of a wife of whom the husband was jealous. This foolish chapter has been the foundation of all appeals to God for the ascertainment of facts, such as the corsned, trial by battle, by water, and by fire, the last of which is our judicial oath. It is very easy to believe that in those days a guilty woman would be afraid to drink the water of jealousy and take the oath, and that, through fear, she might be made to confess. Admitting that the deception tended not only to prevent crime, but to discover it when committed, still, we cannot admit that an honest god would, for any purpose, resort to dishonest means. In all countries fear is employed as a means of getting at the truth, and in this there is nothing dishonest, provided falsehood is not resorted to for the purpose of producing the fear. Protestants laugh at Catholics because of their belief in the efficacy of holy water, and yet they teach their children that a little holy water, in which had been thrown some dust from the floor of the sanctuary, would work a miracle in a woman's flesh.   For hundreds of years our fathers believed that a perjurer could not swallow a piece of sacramental bread.   Such stories belong to the childhood of our race, and are now believed only by mental infants and intellectual babes.

I cannot believe that Moses had in his hands a couple of tables of stone, upon which God had written the Ten Commandments, and that when he saw the golden calf, and the dancing, that he dashed the tables to the earth and broke them in pieces. Neither do I believe that Moses took a golden calf, burnt it, ground it to powder, and made the people drink it with water, as related in the thirty-second chapter of Exodus.

There is another account of the giving of the Ten Commandments to Moses, in the nineteenth and twentieth chapters of Exodus.   In this account not one word is said about the people having made a golden calf, nor about the breaking of the tables of stone.   In the thirty-fourth chapter of Exodus, there is an account of the renewal of the broken tables of the law, and the commandments are given, but they are not the same commandments mentioned in the

twentieth chapter.   There are two accounts of the
same transaction.   Both of these stories cannot be
true, and yet both must be believed.   Any one who
will take the trouble to read the nineteenth and
twentieth chapters, and the last verse of the thirty-
first chapter, the thirty-second, thirty-third, and
thirty-fourth chapters of Exodus, will be compelled
to admit that both accounts cannot be true.

From the last account it appears that while Moses
was upon Mount Sinai receiving the commandments
from God, the people brought their jewelry to Aaron
and he cast for them a golden calf.   This happened
before any commandment against idolatry had been
given.   A god ought, certainly, to publish his laws
before inflicting penalties for their violation.   To
inflict punishment for breaking unknown and un-
published laws is, in the last degree, cruel and
unjust.   It may be replied that the Jews knew better
than to worship idols, before the law was given.   If
this is so, why should the law have been given?   In
all civilized countries, laws are made and pro-
mulgated, not simply for the purpose of informing
the people as to what is right and wrong, but to
inform them of the penalties to be visited upon those
who violate the laws.   When the Ten Command-

ments were given, no penalties were attached.   Not one word was written on the tables of stone as to the punishments that would be inflicted for breaking any or all of the inspired laws.   The people should not have been punished for violating a commandment before it was given.   And yet, in this case, Moses commanded the sons of Levi to take their swords and slay every man his brother, his companion, and his neighbor.   The brutal order was obeyed, and three thousand men were butchered.   The Levites consecrated themselves unto the Lord by murdering their sons, and their brothers, for having violated a commandment before it had been given.

It has been contended for many years that the Ten Commandments are the foundation of all ideas of justice and of law.   Eminent jurists have bowed to popular prejudice, and deformed their works by statements to the effect that the Mosaic laws are the fountains from which sprang all ideas of right and wrong.   Nothing can be more stupidly false than such assertions.   Thousands of years before Moses was born, the Egyptians had a code of laws.   They had laws against blasphemy, murder, adultery, larceny, perjury, laws for the collection of debts, the enforcement of contracts, the ascertainment of damages, the redemption of property pawned, and upon nearly every subject of human interest. The Egyptian code was far better than the Mosaic.

Laws spring from the instinct of self-preservation. Industry objected to supporting idleness, and laws were made against theft. Laws were made against murder, because a very large majority of the people have always objected to being murdered. All fundamental laws were born simply of the instinct of self-defence. Long before the Jewish savages assembled at the foot of Sinai, laws had been made and enforced, not only in Egypt and India, but by every tribe that ever existed.

It is impossible for human beings to exist together, without certain rules of conduct, certain ideas of the proper and improper, of the right and wrong, growing out of the relation. Certain rules must be made, and must be enforced. This implies law, trial and punishment. Whoever produces anything by weary labor, does not need a revelation from heaven to teach him that he has a right to the thing produced. Not one of the learned gentlemen who pretend that the Mosaic laws are filled with justice and intelligence, would live, for a moment, in any country where such laws were in force.

Nothing can be more wonderful than the medical ideas of Jehovah. He had the strangest notions about the cause and cure of disease. With him everything was miracle and wonder. In the fourteenth chapter of Leviticus, we find the law for cleansing a leper :—" Then shall the priest take for him that is to be cleansed, two birds, alive and clean, and cedar wood, and scarlet, and hyssop. And the priest shall command that one of the birds be killed in an *earthen* vessel, over *running* water. As for the living bird, he shall take it, and the cedar wood, and the scarlet, and the hyssop, and shall dip them, and the living bird, in the blood of the bird that was killed over the running water. And he shall sprinkle upon him that is to be cleansed from the leprosy, seven times, and shall pronounce him clean, and shall let the living bird loose into the open field."

We are told that God himself gave these directions to Moses. Does anybody believe this? Why should the bird be killed in an *earthen* vessel? Would the charm be broken if the vessel was of wood? Why over *running* water? What would be thought of a physician now, who would give a prescription like that?

Is it not strange that God, although he gave hundreds of directions for the purpose of discovering the presence of leprosy, and for cleansing the leper after he was healed, forgot to tell how that disease could be cured? Is it not wonderful that while God told his people what animals were fit for food, he failed to give a list of plants that man might eat? Why did he leave his children to find out the hurtful and the poisonous by experiment, knowing that experiment, in millions of cases, must be death?

When reading the history of the Jewish people, of their flight from slavery to death, of their exchange of tyrants, I must confess that my sympathies are all aroused in their behalf. They were cheated, deceived and abused. Their god was quick-tempered, unreasonable, cruel, revengeful and dishonest. He was always promising but never performed. He wasted time in ceremony and childish detail, and in the exaggeration of what he had done. It is impossible for me to conceive of a character more utterly detestable than that of the Hebrew god. He had solemnly promised the Jews that he would take them from Egypt to a land flowing with milk and honey. He had led them to believe that in a little while their troubles would be over, and that they would soon in the land of Canaan, surrounded by their wives and little ones, forget the stripes and tears of Egypt. After promising the poor wanderers again and again that he would lead them in safety to the promised land of joy and plenty, this God, forgetting every promise, said to the wretches in his power :—" Your carcasses shall fall in this wilderness and your children shall wander until your carcasses be wasted." This curse was the conclusion of the whole matter. Into this dust of death and night faded all the promises of God. Into this rottenness of wandering despair fell all the dreams of liberty and home. Millions of corpses were left to rot in the desert, and each one certified to the dishonesty of Jehovah. I cannot believe these things. They are so cruel and heartless, that my blood is chilled and my sense of justice shocked. A book that is equally abhorrent to my head and heart, cannot be accepted as a revelation from God.

When we think of the poor Jews, destroyed, murdered, bitten by serpents, visited by plagues, decimated by famine, butchered by each other, swallowed by the earth, frightened, cursed, starved, deceived, robbed and outraged, how thankful we should be that we are not the chosen people of

God. No wonder that they longed for the slavery of Egypt, and remembered with sorrow the unhappy day when they exchanged masters. Compared with Jehovah, Pharaoh was a benefactor, and the tyranny of Egypt was freedom to those who suffered the liberty of God.

While reading the Pentateuch, I am filled with indignation, pity and horror. Nothing can be sadder than the history of the starved and frightened wretches who wandered over the desolate crags and sands of wilderness and desert, the prey of famine, sword, and plague. Ignorant and superstitious to the last degree, governed by falsehood, plundered by hypocrisy, they were the sport of priests, and the food of fear. God was their greatest enemy, and death their only friend.

It is impossible to conceive of a more thoroughly despicable, hateful, and arrogant being, than the Jewish god. He is without a redeeming feature. In the mythology of the world he has no parallel. He, only, is never touched by agony and tears. He delights only in blood and pain. Human affections are naught to him. He cares neither for love nor music, beauty nor joy. A false friend, an unjust judge, a braggart, hypocrite, and tyrant, sincere in hatred, jealous, vain, and revengeful, false in promise, honest in curse, suspicious, ignorant, and changeable, infamous and hideous :—such is the God of the Pentateuch.

XXIV.

CONFESS AND AVOID.

THE scientific Christians now admit that the Bible is not inspired in its astronomy, geology, botany, zoology, nor in any science. In other words, they admit that on these subjects, the Bible cannot be depended upon. If all the statements in the Scriptures were true, there would be no necessity for admitting that some of them are not inspired. A Christian will not admit that a passage in the Bible is uninspired, until he is satisfied that it is untrue. Orthodoxy itself has at last been compelled to say, that while a passage may be true and uninspired, it cannot be inspired if false.

If the people of Europe had known as much of astronomy and geology when the Bible was introduced among them, as they do now, there never could have been one believer in the doctrine of inspiration. If the writers of the various parts of the Bible had known as much about the sciences as

is now known by every intelligent man, the book
never could have been written.   It was produced by
ignorance, and has been believed and defended by
its author.   It has lost power in the proportion that
man has gained knowledge.   A few years ago, this
book was appealed to in the settlement of all scientific
questions ; but now, even the clergy confess that in
such matters, it has ceased to speak with the voice
of authority.   For the establishment of facts, the
word of man is now considered far better than the
word of God.   In the world of science, Jehovah was
superseded by Copernicus, Galileo, and Kepler.
All that God told Moses, admitting the entire
account to be true, is dust and ashes compared
to the discoveries of Descartes, Laplace, and
Humboldt.   In matters of fact, the Bible has ceased
to be regarded as a standard.   Science has succeeded
in breaking the chains of theology.   A few years
ago, Science endeavored to show that it was not
inconsistent with the Bible.   The tables have been
turned, and now, Religion is endeavoring to prove
that the Bible is not inconsistent with Science.   The
standard has been changed.

For many ages, the Christians contended that the
Bible, viewed simply as a literary performance, was

beyond all other books, and that man without the assistance of God could not produce its equal.   This claim was made when but few books existed, and the Bible, being the only book generally known, had no rival.   But this claim, like the other, has been abandoned by many, and soon will be, by all.   Compared with Shakespeare's "book and volume of the brain," the "sacred" Bible shrinks and seems as feebly impotent and vain, as would a pipe of Pan, when some great organ, voiced with every tone, from the hoarse thunder of the sea to the winged warble of a mated bird, floods and fills cathedral aisles with all the wealth of sound.

It is now maintained—and this appears to be the last fortification behind which the doctrine of inspiration skulks and crouches—that the Bible, although false and mistaken in its astronomy, geology, geography, history and philosophy, is inspired in its morality.   It is now claimed that had it not been for this book, the world would have been inhabited only by savages, and that had it not been for the Holy Scriptures, man never would have even dreamed of the unity of God.   A belief in one God is claimed to be a dogma of almost infinite importance, that without this belief civilization is impossible, and that this

fact is the sun around which all the virtues revolve
For my part, I think it infinitely more important
to believe in man. Theology is a superstition
—Humanity a religion.

XXV.

"INSPIRED" SLAVERY.

PERHAPS the Bible was inspired upon the subject of human slavery. Is there, in the civilized world, to-day, a clergyman who believes in the divinity of slavery? Does the Bible teach man to enslave his brother? If it does, is it not blasphemous to say that it is inspired of God? If you find the institution of slavery upheld in a book said to have been written by God, what would you expect to find in a book inspired by the devil? Would you expect to find that book in favor of liberty? Modern Christians, ashamed of the God of the Old Testament, endeavor now to show that slavery was neither commanded nor opposed by Jehovah. Nothing can be plainer than the following passages from the twenty-fifth chapter of Leviticus. "Moreover of the children of the strangers that do sojourn among you, of them shall ye buy, and of their families that are with you, which they begat in your land: and they shall be your possession. And ye shall take them as an inheritance for your children after you, to inherit them for a possession, they shall be your bondmen forever. Both thy bondmen, and thy bondmaids, which thou shalt have, shall be of the heathen that are round about you ; of them shall ye buy bondmen, and bondmaids."

Can we believe in this, the Nineteenth Century, that these infamous passages were inspired by God? that God approved not only of human slavery, but instructed his chosen people to buy the women, children and babes of the heathen round about them ? If it was right for the Hebrews to buy, it was also right for the heathen to sell. This God, by commanding the Hebrews to buy, approved of the selling of sons and daughters. The Canaanite who, tempted by gold, lured by avarice, sold from the arms of his wife the dimpled babe, simply made it possible for the Hebrews to obey the orders of their God. If God is the author of the Bible, the reading of these passages ought to cover his cheeks with shame. I ask the Christian world to-day, was it right for the heathen to sell their children ? Was it right for God not only to uphold, but to command the infamous traffic in human flesh ? Could the most revengeful fiend, the most malicious vagrant in the gloom of hell, sink to a lower moral depth than this ?

According to this God, his chosen people were not only commanded to buy of the heathen round about them, but were also permitted to buy each other for a term of years.   The law governing the purchase of Jews is laid down in the twenty-first chapter of Exodus.   " If thou buy a Hebrew servant, six years shall he serve : and in the seventh he shall go out free for nothing.   If he came in by himself, he shall go out by himself : if he were married, then his wife shall go out with him.   If his master have given him a wife, and she have borne him sons or daughters, the wife and her children shall be her master's, and he shall go out by himself.   And if the servant shall plainly say, I love my master, my wife, and my children ; I will not go out free :   Then his master shall bring him unto the judges ; he shall also bring him to the door, or unto the door-post : and his master shall bore his ear through with an awl : and he shall serve him forever."

Do you believe that God was the author of this infamous law ?   Do you believe that the loving father of us all, turned the dimpled arms of babes into manacles of iron ?   Do you believe that he baited the dungeon of servitude with wife and child ? Is it possible to love a God who would make such laws ?   Is it possible not to hate and despise him ?

The heathen are not spoken of as human beings. Their rights are never mentioned.   They were the rightful food of the sword, and their bodies were made for stripes and chains.

In the same chapter of the same inspired book, we are told that, " if a man smite his servant, or his maid, with a rod, and he dies under his hand, he shall be surely punished.   Notwithstanding, if he continue a day or two, he shall not be punished, for he is his money."

Must we believe that God called some of his children the money of others ?   Can we believe that God made lashes upon the naked back, a legal tender for labor performed ?   Must we regard the auction block as an altar ?   Were blood hounds apostles ?   Was the slave-pen a temple ?   Were the stealers and whippers of babes and women the justified children of God ?

It is now contended that while the Old Testament is touched with the barbarism of its time, that the New Testament is morally perfect, and that on its pages can be found no blot or stain. As a matter of fact, the New Testament is more decidedly in favor of human slavery than the old.

For my part, I never will, I never can, worship a God who upholds the institution of slavery. Such a God I hate and defy. I neither want his heaven, nor fear his hell.

XXVI.

"INSPIRED" MARRIAGE.

Is there an orthodox clergyman in the world, who will now declare that he believes the institution of polygamy to be right? Is there one who will publicly declare that, in his judgment, that institution ever was right? Was there ever a time in the history of the world when it was right to treat woman simply as property? Do not attempt to answer these questions by saying, that the Bible is an exceedingly good book, that we are indebted for our civilization to the sacred volume, and that without it, man would lapse into savagery, and mental night. This is no answer. Was there a time when the institution of polygamy was the highest expression of human virtue? Is there a Christian woman, civilized, intelligent, and free, who believes in the institution of polygamy? Are we better, purer, and more intelligent than God was four thousand years ago? Why should we imprison Mormons, and worship God? Polygamy is just as pure in Utah, as it could have been in the promised land. Love and Virtue are the same the whole world round, and Justice is the same in every star. All the languages of the world are not sufficient to express the filth of polygamy. It makes of man, a beast, of woman, a trembling slave. It destroys the fireside, makes virtue an outcast, takes from human speech its sweetest words, and leaves the heart a den, where crawl and hiss the slimy serpents of most loathsome lust. Civilization rests upon the family. The good family is the unit of good government. The virtues grow about the holy hearth of home—they cluster, bloom, and shed their perfume round the fireside where the one man loves the one woman. Lover— husband—wife—mother—father—child—home!— without these sacred words, the world is but a lair, and men and women merely beasts.

Why should the innocent maiden and the loving mother worship the heartless Jewish God? Why should they, with pure and stainless lips, read the vile record of inspired lust?

The marriage of the one man to the one woman is the citadel and fortress of civilization. Without this, woman becomes the prey and slave of lust and power, and man goes back to savagery and crime. From the bottom of my heart I hate, abhor and execrate all theories of life, of which the pure and sacred home is not the corner-stone. Take from the world the family, the fireside, the children born of wedded love, and there is nothing left. The home where virtue dwells with love is like a lily with a heart of fire—the fairest flower in all the world.

XXVII.

" INSPIRED " WAR.

I F the Bible be true, God commanded his chosen
people to destroy men simply for the crime of
defending their native land.   They were not allowed
to spare trembling and white-haired age, nor dimpled
babes clasped in the mothers' arms.   They were
ordered to kill women, and to pierce, with the sword
of war, the unborn child.   " Our heavenly Father "
commanded the Hebrews to kill the men and women,
the fathers, sons and brothers, but to preserve the
girls alive.   Why were not the maidens also killed ?
Why were they spared ?   Read the thirty-first
chapter of Numbers, and you will find that the
maidens were given to the soldiers and the priests.
Is there, in all the history of war, a more infamous
thing than this ?   Is it possible that God permitted
the violets of modesty, that grow and shed their
perfume in the maiden's heart, to be trampled

beneath the brutal feet of lust? If this was the order of God, what, under the same circumstances, would have been the command of a devil? When, in this age of the world, a woman, a wife, a mother, reads this record, she should, with scorn and loathing, throw the book away. A general, who now should make such an order, giving over to massacre and rapine a conquered people, would be held in execration by the whole civilized world. Yet, if the Bible be true, the supreme and infinite God was once a savage.

A little while ago, out upon the western plains, in a little path leading to a cabin, were found the bodies of two children and their mother. Her breast was filled with wounds received in the defence of her darlings. They had been murdered by the savages. Suppose when looking at their lifeless forms, some one had said, "This was done by the command of God!" In Canaan there were countless scenes like this. There was no pity in inspired war. God raised the black flag, and commanded his soldiers to kill even the smiling infant in its mother's arms. Who is the blasphemer; the man who denies the existence of God, or he who covers the robes of the Infinite with innocent blood?

We are told in the Pentateuch, that God, the father of us all, gave thousands of maidens, after having killed their fathers, their mothers, and their brothers, to satisfy the brutal lusts of savage men. If there be a God, I pray him to write in his book, opposite my name, that I denied this lie for him.

XXVIII.

"INSPIRED" RELIGIOUS LIBERTY.

ACCORDING to the Bible, God selected the Jewish people through whom to make known the great fact, that he was the only true and living God. For this purpose, he appeared on several occasions to Moses—came down to Sinai's top clothed in cloud and fire, and wrought a thousand miracles for the preservation and education of the Jewish people. In their presence he opened the waters of the sea. For them he caused bread to rain from heaven. To quench their thirst, water leaped from the dry and barren rock. Their enemies were miraculously destroyed ; and for forty years, at least, this God took upon himself the government of the Jews. But, after all this, many of the people had less confidence in him than in gods of wood and stone. In moments of trouble, in periods of disaster, in the darkness of doubt, in the hunger and thirst of famine, instead of asking this God for aid, they turned and sought the help of senseless things. This God, with all his power and wisdom, could not even convince a few wandering and wretched savages that he was more potent than the idols of Egypt. This God was not willing that the Jews should think and investigate for themselves. For heresy, the penalty was death. Where this God reigned, intellectual liberty was unknown. He appealed only to brute force ; he collected taxes by threatening plagues ; he demanded worship on pain of sword and fire ; acting as spy, inquisitor, judge and executioner.

In the thirteenth chapter of Deuteronomy, we have the ideas of God as to mental freedom. " If thy brother, the son of thy mother, or thy son, or the wife of thy bosom, or thy friend which is as thine own soul, entice thee secretly, saying, Let us go and serve other gods, which thou hast not known, thou nor thy fathers ; *namely* of the gods of the people which are around about you, nigh unto thee, or far off from thee, from the one end of the earth even unto the other end of the earth, Thou shalt not consent unto him, nor hearken unto him, neither shall thine eye pity him, neither shalt thou spare him, neither shalt thou conceal him. But thou shalt surely kill him ; thine hand shall be first upon him to put him to death, and afterward the hand of all the people. And thou shalt stone him with stones that he die."

This is the religious liberty of God; the toleration of Jehovah. If I had lived in Palestine at that time, and my wife, the mother of my children, had said to me, "I am tired of Jehovah, he is always asking for blood; he is never weary of killing; he is always telling of his might and strength; always telling what he has done for the Jews, always asking for sacrifices; for doves and lambs—blood, nothing but blood.—Let us worship the sun. Jehovah is too revengeful, too malignant, too exacting. Let us worship the sun. The sun has clothed the world in beauty; it has covered the earth with flowers; by its divine light I first saw your face, and my beautiful babe."—If I had obeyed the command of God, I would have killed her. My hand would have been first upon her, and after that the hands of all the people, and she would have been stoned with stones until she died. For my part, I would never kill my wife, even if commanded so to do by the real God of this universe. Think of taking up some ragged rock and hurling it against the white bosom filled with love for you; and when you saw oozing from the bruised lips of the death wound, the red current of her sweet life—think of looking up to heaven and receiving the congratulations of the infinite fiend whose commandment you had obeyed!

Can we believe that any such command was ever given by a merciful and intelligent God?   Suppose, however, that God did give this law to the Jews, and did tell them that whenever a man preached a heresy, or proposed to worship any other God that they should kill him ; and suppose that afterward this same God took upon himself flesh, and came to this very chosen people and taught a different religion, and that thereupon the Jews crucified him ; I ask you, did he not reap exactly what he had sown ? What right would this God have to complain of a crucifixion suffered in accordance with his own command?

Nothing can be more infamous than intellectual tyranny.   To put chains upon the body is as nothing compared with putting shackles on the brain.   No god is entitled to the worship or the respect of man who does not give, even to the meanest of his children, every right that he claims for himself.

If the Pentateuch be true, religious persecution is a duty.   The dungeons of the Inquisition were temples, and the clank of every chain upon the limbs of heresy was music in the ear of God.   If the Pentateuch was inspired, every heretic should be destroyed ; and every man who advocates a fact inconsistent with the sacred book, should be consumed by sword and flame.

In the Old Testament no one is told to reason with a heretic, and not one word is said about relying upon argument, upon education, nor upon intellectual development—nothing except simple brute force.   Is there to-day a Christian who will say that four thousand years ago, it was the duty of a husband to kill his wife if she differed with him upon the subject of religion ?   Is there one who will now say that, under such circumstances, the wife ought to have been killed ?   Why should God be so jealous of the wooden idols of the heathen ?   Could he not compete with Baal ?   Was he envious of the success of the Egyptian magicians ?   Was it not possible for him to make such a convincing display of his power as to silence forever the voice of unbelief?   Did this God have to resort to force to make converts ?   Was he so ignorant of the structure of the human mind as to believe all honest doubt a crime ?   If he wished to do away with the idolatry of the Canaanites, why did he not appear to them? Why did he not give them the tables of the law? Why did he only make known his will to a few wandering savages in the desert of Sinai? Will some theologian have the kindness to answer these questions? Will some minister, who now believes in religious liberty, and eloquently denounces the intolerance of Catholicism, explain these things; will he tell us why he worships an intolerant God? Is a god who will burn a soul forever in another world, better than a Christian who burns the body for a few hours in this? Is there no intellectual liberty in heaven? Do the angels all discuss questions on the same side? Are all the investigators in perdition? Will the penitent thief, winged and crowned, laugh at the honest folks in hell? Will the agony of the damned increase or decrease the happiness of God? Will there be, in the universe, an eternal *auto da fe* ?

XXIX.

CONCLUSION.

IF the Pentateuch is not inspired in its astronomy, geology, geography, history or philosophy, if it is not inspired concerning slavery, polygamy, war, law, religious or political liberty, or the rights of men, women and children, what is it inspired in, or about? The unity of God?—that was believed long before Moses was born. Special providence?—that has been the doctrine of ignorance in all ages. The rights of property?—theft was always a crime. The sacrifice of animals?—that was a custom thousands of years before a Jew existed. The sacredness of life?—there have always been laws against murder. The wickedness of perjury?—truthfulness has always been a virtue. The beauty of chastity?—the Pentateuch does not teach it. Thou shalt worship no other God?—that has been the burden of all religions.

Is it possible that the Pentateuch could not have been written by uninspired men? that the assistance of God was necessary to produce these books? Is it possible that Galileo ascertained the mechanical principles of "Virtual Velocity," the laws of falling bodies and of all motion; that Copernicus ascertained the true position of the earth and accounted for all celestial phenomena; that Kepler discovered his three laws—discoveries of such importance that the 8th of May, 1618, may be called the birthday of modern science; that Newton gave to the world the Method of Fluxions, the Theory of Universal Gravitation, and the Decomposition of Light; that Euclid, Cavalieri, Descartes, and Leibnitz, almost completed the science of mathematics; that all the discoveries in optics, hydrostatics, pneumatics and chemistry, the experiments, discoveries, and inventions of Galvani, Volta, Franklin and Morse, of Trevethick, Watt and Fulton and of all the pioneers of progress—that all this was accomplished by uninspired men, while the writer of the Pentateuch was directed and inspired by an infinite God? Is it possible that the codes of China, India, Egypt, Greece and Rome were made by man, and that the laws recorded in the Pentateuch were alone given by

God?   Is it possible that Æschylus and Shakespeare,
Burns, and Beranger, Goethe and Schiller, and all the
poets of the world, and all their wondrous tragedies
and songs, are but the work of men, while no intelligence except the infinite God could be the author
of the Pentateuch ?   Is it possible that of all the
books that crowd the libraries of the world, the
books of science, fiction, history and song, that all
save only one, have been produced by man ?   Is it
possible that of all these, the Bible only is the work
of God ?

If the Pentateuch is inspired, the civilization of
our day is a mistake and crime.   There should be
no political liberty.   Heresy should be trodden out
beneath the bigot's brutal feet.   Husbands should
divorce their wives at will, and make the mothers of
their children houseless and weeping wanderers.
Polygamy ought to be practiced ; women should become slaves ; we should buy the sons and daughters
of the heathen and make them bondmen and bond-
women forever.   We should sell our own flesh and
blood, and have the right to kill our slaves.   Men
and women should be stoned to death for laboring
on the seventh day.   " Mediums," such as have
familiar spirits, should be burned with fire.   Every

vestige of mental liberty should be destroyed, and reason's holy torch extinguished in the martyr's blood.

Is it not far better and wiser to say that the Pentateuch while containing some good laws, some truths, some wise and useful things is, after all, deformed and blackened by the savagery of its time? Is it not far better and wiser to take the good and throw the bad away?

Let us admit what we know to be true; that Moses was mistaken about a thousand things; that the story of creation is not true; that the Garden of Eden is a myth; that the serpent and the tree of knowledge, and the fall of man are but fragments of old mythologies lost and dead; that woman was not made out of a rib; that serpents never had the power of speech; that the sons of God did not marry the daughters of men; that the story of the flood and ark is not exactly true; that the tower of Babel is a mistake; that the confusion of tongues is a childish thing; that the origin of the rainbow is a foolish fancy; that Methuselah did not live nine hundred and sixty-nine years; that Enoch did not leave this world, taking with him his flesh and bones; that the story of Sodom and Gomorrah is somewhat

improbable ; that burning brimstone never fell like
rain : that Lot's wife was not changed into chloride
of sodium ; that Jacob did not, in fact, put his hip
out of joint wrestling with God ; that the history of
Tamar might just as well have been left out ; that a
belief in Pharaoh's dreams is not essential to salvation ; that it makes but little difference whether the
rod of Aaron was changed to a serpent or not ; that
of all the wonders said to have been performed in
Egypt, the greatest is, that anybody ever believed
the absurd account ; that God did not torment the
innocent cattle on account of the sins of their owners ;
that he did not kill the first born of the poor maid
behind the mill because of Pharaoh's crimes ; that
flies and frogs were not ministers of God's wrath ;
that lice and locusts were not the executors of his
will ; that seventy people did not, in two hundred
and fifteen years, increase to three million ; that
three priests could not eat six hundred pigeons in a
day ; that gazing at a brass serpent could not extract
poison from the blood ; that God did not go in
partnership with hornets ; that he did not murder
people simply because they asked for something to
eat ; that he did not declare the making of hair oil
and ointment an offence to be punished with death ;

that he did not miraculously preserve cloth and
leather ; that he was not afraid of wild beasts ; that
he did not punish heresy with sword and fire ; that
he was not jealous, revengeful, and unjust ; that he
knew all about the sun, moon, and stars ; that he
did not threaten to kill people for eating the fat of
an ox ; that he never told Aaron to draw cuts to see
which of two goats should be killed ; that he never
objected to clothes made of woolen mixed with linen ;
that if he objected to dwarfs, people with flat noses
and too many fingers, he ought not to have created
such folks ; that he did not demand human sacrifices
as set forth in the last chapter of Leviticus ; that he
did not object to the raising of horses ; that he never
commanded widows to spit in the faces of their
brothers-in-law ; that several contradictory accounts
of the same transaction cannot all be true ; that God
did not talk to Abraham as one man talks to another ;
that angels were not in the habit of walking about
the earth eating veal dressed with milk and butter,
and making bargains about the destruction of cities ;
that God never turned himself into a flame of fire,
and lived in a bush ; that he never met Moses in a
hotel and tried to kill him ; that it was absurd to
perform miracles to induce a king to act in a certain

way and then harden his heart so that he would
refuse ; that God was not kept from killing the Jews
by the fear that the Egyptians would laugh at him ;
that he did not secretly bury a man and then allow
the corpse to write an account of the funeral ; that he
never believed the firmament to be solid ; that he
knew slavery was and always would be a frightful
crime ; that polygamy is but stench and filth ; that
the brave soldier will always spare an unarmed foe ;
that only cruel cowards slay the conquered and the
helpless ; that no language can describe the murderer
of a smiling babe ; that God did not want the blood
of doves and lambs ; that he did not love the smell of
burning flesh ; that he did not want his altars daubed
with blood ; that he did not pretend that the sins of
a people could be transferred to a goat ; that he did
not believe in witches, wizards, spooks, and devils ;
that he did not test the virtue of woman with dirty
water ; that he did not suppose that rabbits chewed
the cud ; that he never thought there were any four-
footed birds ; that he did not boast for several
hundred years that he had vanquished an Egyptian
king ; that a dry stick did not bud, blossom, and
bear almonds in one night ; that manna did not
shrink and swell, so that each man could gather only

just one omer ; that it was never wrong to "coun-
tenance the poor man in his cause ; " that God never
told a people not to live in peace with their neighbors;
that he did not spend forty days with Moses on
Mount Sinai giving him patterns for making clothes,
tongs, basins, and snuffers ; that maternity is not a
sin ; that physical deformity is not a crime ; that
an atonement cannot be made for the soul by
shedding innocent blood ; that killing a dove over
running water will not make its blood a medicine ;
that a god who demands love knows nothing of
the human heart ; that one who frightens savages
with loud noises is unworthy the love of civilized
men ; that one who destroys children on account of
the sins of their fathers is a monster ; that an infinite
god never threatened to give people the itch ; that
he never sent wild beasts to devour babes ; that he
never ordered the violation of maidens ; that he
never regarded patriotism as a crime ; that he never
ordered the destruction of unborn children ; that he
never opened the earth and swallowed wives and
babes because husbands and fathers had displeased
him ; that he never demanded that men should kill
their sons and brothers, for the purpose of sanctifying
themselves ; that we cannot please God by believing

the improbable ; that credulity is not a virtue ; that investigation is not a crime ; that every mind should be free ; that all religious persecution is infamous in God, as well as man ; that without liberty, virtue is impossible ; that without freedom, even love cannot exist ; that every man should be allowed to think and to express his thoughts ; that woman is the equal of man ; that children should be governed by love and reason ; that the family relation is sacred ; that war is a hideous crime ; that all intolerance is born of ignorance and hate ; that the freedom of to-day is the hope of to-morrow ; that the enlightened present ought not to fall upon its knees and blindly worship the barbaric past ; and that every free, brave and enlightened man should publicly declare that all the ignorant, infamous, heartless, hideous things recorded in the "inspired" Pentateuch are not the words of God, but simply " Some Mistakes of Moses."

PAPERBACKS AVAILABLE FROM PROMETHEUS BOOKS

SCIENCE AND THE PARANORMAL

____ 12.95 Ancient Astronauts, Cosmic Collisions *William Stiebing, Jr.*
____ 11.95 The Bermuda Triangle Mystery—Solved *Larry Kusche*
____ 13.95 ESP and Parapsychology *C. E. M. Hansel*
____ 11.95 Flim-Flam! *James Randi*
____ 12.95 The Fringe of the Unknown *L. Sprague de Camp*
____ 12.95 The Gemini Syndrome *Culver and Ianna*
____ 11.95 The Loch Ness Mystery Solved *Ronald Binns*
____ 16.95 Paranormal Borderlands of Science *edited by Kendrick Frazier*
____ 13.95 Psychic Paradoxes *John Booth*
____ 13.95 The Psychology of the Psychic *Marks and Kammann*
____ 15.95 Science Confronts the Paranormal *edited by Kendrick Frazier*
____ 16.95 A Skeptic's Handbook of Parapsychology *edited by Paul Kurtz*
____ 13.95 The Spiritualists *Ruth Brandon*
____ 10.95 The Truth About Uri Geller *James Randi*
____ 11.95 UFOs: The Public Deceived *Philip J. Klass*
____ 13.95 The UFO Verdict *Robert Sheaffer*

PHILOSOPHY

____ 11.95 Animal Rights and Human Morality *Bernard Rollin*
____ 10.95 The Art of Deception *Nicholas Capaldi*
____ 17.95 Business Ethics *edited by Snoeyenbos, Almeder, and Humber*
____ 17.95 Contemporary Analytic and Linguistic Philosophies *edited by E. D. Klemke*
____ 17.95 Contemporary Readings in Social and Political Ethics *edited by Brodsky, Troyer, and Vance*
____ 16.95 Decisions in Philosophy of Religion *William B. Williamson*
____ 13.95 Esthetics Contemporary *edited by Richard Kostelanetz*
____ 16.95 Ethics and the Legal Profession *edited by Davis and Elliston*
____ 17.95 Ethics and the Search for Values *edited by Navia and Kelly*
____ 9.95 Ethics Without God *Kai Nielsen*
____ 10.95 Exuberance *Paul Kurtz*
____ 11.95 Good and Evil *Richard Taylor*
____ 14.95 An Invitation to Philosophy *edited by Capaldi, Kelly, and Navia*
____ 17.95 Journeys Through Philosophy (Revised) *edited by Capaldi, Navia, and Kelly*
____ 15.95 Latin American Philosophy in the Twentieth Century *edited by Jorge J. E. Gracia*
____ 3.95 On Liberty *John Stuart Mill*
____ 10.95 Philosophy: An Introduction *Antony Flew*
____ 15.95 Philosophy and Science Fiction *edited by Michael Philips*
____ 16.95 Philosophy and Sex (Revised) *edited by Baker and Elliston*
____ 4.95 The Politics *Aristotle*
____ 4.95 The Prince *Niccolo Machiavelli*
____ 11.95 The Problem of God *Peter A. Angeles*
____ 5.95 The Republic *Plato*
____ 3.95 The Second Treatise on Civil Government *John Locke*
____ 3.95 The Subjection of Women *John Stuart Mill*
____ 9.95 Thinking Straight *Antony Flew*
____ 11.95 The Worlds of the Early Greek Philosophers *edited by Wilbur and Allen*
____ 11.95 The Worlds of Hume and Kant *edited by Wilbur and Allen*
____ 11.95 The Worlds of Plato and Aristotle *edited by Wilbur and Allen*

POPULAR SCIENCE

____ 12.95 In the Beginning *Chris McGowan*
____ 12.95 The Magic Numbers of Dr. Matrix *Martin Gardner*
____ 11.95 The Roving Mind *Isaac Asimov*

SOCIAL SCIENCES AND CURRENT EVENTS

HEALTH ISSUES

NEW CONCEPTS IN HUMAN SEXUALITY

LITERATURE, CRITICISM AND BIOGRAPHY

FRONTIERS IN EDUCATION

THE SKEPTIC'S BOOKSHELF

_____ 10.95 The Age of Reason *Thomas Paine*
_____ 15.95 An Anthology of Atheism and Rationalism *edited by Gordon Stein*
_____ 10.95 Atheism: The Case Against God *George H. Smith*
_____ 8.95 The Atheist Debater's Handbook *B. C. Johnson*
_____ 12.95 Bertrand Russell on God and Religion *edited by Al Seckel*
_____ 13.95 Judaism Beyond God: A Radical New Way to Be Jewish *Sherwin T. Wine*
_____ 11.95 The Mystery of the Kingdom of God *Albert Schweitzer*
_____ 15.95 The Origins of Christianity *R. Joseph Hoffmann*
_____ 12.95 Some Mistakes of Moses *Robert G. Ingersoll*

HUMANISM

_____ 11.95 The Best of Robert Ingersoll *edited by Roger E. Greeley*
_____ 7.95 The Humanist Alternative *edited by Paul Kurtz*
_____ 12.95 Humanist Ethics *edited by Morris B. Storer*
_____ 6.95 A Humanist Funeral Service *Corliss Lamont*
_____ 2.95 Humanist Manifestos I and II
_____ 3.95 A Humanist Wedding Service *Corliss Lamont*
_____ 10.95 In Defense of Secular Humanism *Paul Kurtz*
_____ 2.95 A Secular Humanist Declaration

The books listed above can be obtained from your book dealer or directly from Prometheus Books. Please check off the appropriate books. Remittance must accompany all orders from individuals. Please include $2.00 postage and handling for first book, .75 for each additional book (4.50 maximum). (N.Y.S. residents please add applicable sales tax.)

Send to _____
(Please type or print clearly)
Address _____
City _____ State _____ Zip _____
Charge my ☐ **VISA**   Amount Enclosed _____
             ☐ **MasterCard**
Acct. _____   Phone orders (outside NYS) call toll free: 800-421-0351.
Exp. Date _____ Tel. # _____   In NYS: 716-837-2475
Signature _____   Please allow 3-6 weeks for delivery

PROMETHEUS BOOKS
700 E. Amherst Street, Buffalo, NY 14215